3.95

CHRISTMAS DECORATIONS
FROM WILLIAMSBURG'S FOLK
ART COLLECTION

Christmas Decorations from Williamsburg's Folk Art Collection

STEP-BY-STEP ILLUSTRATED INSTRUCTIONS FOR
CHRISTMAS ORNAMENTS THAT CAN BE MADE AT HOME

Compiled and adapted
by the staff of the
Abby Aldrich Rockefeller
Folk Art Collection

Photographs by Frank Davis
Line Drawings by Louis Luedtke

Published by
THE COLONIAL WILLIAMSBURG FOUNDATION · Williamsburg, Virginia

Distributed by
HOLT, RINEHART AND WINSTON · New York, New York

Library of Congress Cataloging in Publication Data

Main entry under title:

Christmas decorations from Williamsburg's folk art
   collection.

   1. Christmas decorations. 2. Folk art—Virginia—
Williamsburg. I. Abby Aldrich Rockefeller Folk Art
Collection, Williamsburg, Va.
TT900.C4C46   745.59'41   76-41253
ISBN 0-87935-037-7
ISBN 0-87935-040-7 pbk.

ISBN 0-03-018816-4 (Holt, Rinehart & Winston) hardbd
      0-87935-037-7 (Colonial Williamsburg) hardbd
      0-87935-040-7 (Colonial Williamsburg) softbd

Proceeds from the sale of this book will be applied
to future publications on American folk art.

PRINTED IN THE UNITED STATES OF AMERICA

Contents

Needlework

Paper

Wood

Other

Introduction

WILLIAMSBURG'S FOLK ART COLLECTION was established by Abby Aldrich Rockefeller in 1939. Mrs. Rockefeller hoped that by giving wider exposure to her pioneer collection of weathervanes, trade signs, and unsophisticated paintings, more people would recognize the aesthetic quality in the best of this material and would begin to appreciate and enjoy the creative efforts of American artists and craftspeople who had not been exposed to formal art training. Her original gift of 424 objects has become the nucleus of the nation's most active folk art museum, which houses a collection that now numbers some 2,000 items and continues to grow through gifts and purchases.

In recent years, the Abby Aldrich Rockefeller Folk Art Collection has earned widespread recognition for its imaginative annual Christmas shows. Various folk art forms are displayed in light-hearted exhibits that suggest some of the customs and traditions associated with an old-fashioned American Christmas. A floor-to-ceiling tree trimmed with homemade decorations made by friends of the museum is always a focal point.

The custom of trimming a Christmas tree was introduced to Williamsburg in 1842, when Charles Minnegerode, a German immigrant teaching at the College of William and Mary, shared a cherished tradition of his youth by decorating a little tree for the children of his friend and colleague, Professor Nathaniel Beverley Tucker.

Tree trimming was not widely practiced in the United States until after the Civil War. Here, as abroad, the first trees were small enough to be set on tables. Initially, Christmas trees were hung with edibles, but by 1860 city folk could purchase special toys and imported glass ornaments. Families living in rural areas exercised their ingenuity and contrived tree ornaments out of spare materials. Favorite decorations included candles, cookies, popcorn strings, gilded walnuts, candy filled cornucopias, blown and colored eggs, paper chains and cut outs, baskets, small flags, simple toys, carvings, and little gifts. Because of their ephemeral nature, very few examples of homemade nineteenth-century Christmas tree decorations survive.

Lately, Bicentennial activities have awakened a new awareness of heritage and tradition, reminding us of a time when life was less complex and commercial and more centered on family and community. The urge to take the tinsel out of Christmas gained new impetus in 1975 when, at Mrs. Betty Ford's request, Williamsburg's Folk Art Collection provided 3,000 decorations for the White House tree. About two-thirds of the tree trims were made by Colonial Williamsburg staff and local people. Word of the project traveled to friends across the country, and they also sent things. Contributors were urged to be as creative and imaginative as possible in combining natural, inexpensive materials. The result was a diverse assortment of unusually attractive homemade ornaments, many based on folk crafts.

The publicity given the White House project produced a flood of requests from individuals who wanted directions for duplicating the tree ornaments, and the Folk Art Collection staff has responded with this book. It is meant for people of all ages who enjoy working with their hands. Every effort has been made to provide easy-to-follow, accurate directions and to include only decorations that are within the ability of anyone willing to master a few simple techniques. Naturally, the needlepoint, crocheted, knitted, and carved decorations require a basic understanding of these skills.

All of the ornaments can be made from relatively inexpensive materials that are readily found about the house or are available nearby. Substitutions are encouraged, and readers are urged to improvise and experiment. Our back-to-basics approach calls for such natural things as nuts, dried materials, straw, pinecones, feathers, and seashells, which can be combined with scraps of fabric, yarn, and ribbon. To preserve a traditional look, the use of foil, sequins, and glitter is discouraged.

Although cones can be found in wooded areas in any season and bird feathers are always around, readers are warned that it may require a bit of planning to procure some of the materials necessary for making the decorations. Summer trips to the beach are a good time to collect shells, starfish, and sand dollars. Vacation travels may take you to areas where unusual seed pods, cones, and nuts are yours for the gathering. Straw needs to be cut between May and August, depending on the region, while shucks and cobs from field corn, berries, red peppers, acorns, peanuts, and most of the other natural materials required are plentiful in early fall.

The ideas for these decorations have been submitted by friends of the Abby Aldrich Rockefeller Folk Art Collection over a four-year period, and the contributor's name accompanies each entry. Selection was made by the museum staff. Catherine Gibbons, project coordinator, compiled the directions, assisted by Gail Andrews and Ann Barton Brown. Each set of instructions was tested by Susan H. Rountree, with occasional help from son Jeffrey, age 7. The charming step-by-step drawings are from the pen of Louis Luedtke, a talented Williamsburg artist. Frank Davis, a staff photographer for the Colonial Williamsburg Foundation, provided the color and black and white pictures.

It is impossible to list here the many kind individuals who have assisted with this project at various times and in different ways, but I am grateful to them all. I would also like to express my appreciation and apologies to those whose decoration ideas could not be included because of lack of space. And my special thanks to Judith W. Blood, whose enthusiasm for Christmas is boundless. Happily it is also contagious!

BEATRIX T. RUMFORD
Director, Abby Aldrich Rockefeller Folk Art Collection

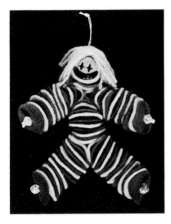

FELT CLOWN

1 red and 1 white piece of felt, each 8
   x 9 inches
Scissors
Heavy thread
Large needle
4 ¼-inch round beads
1-inch wooden bead, white or
   unpainted
58 ¼-inch wooden beads

Small flat wooden bead
Yellow yarn
Household cement
Tiny, pointed brush
Red paint
Black indelible felt pen with a fine
   point.

Cut out 32 1-inch circles of the red felt and 32 of the white. Thread the needle with heavy thread.

Legs—Both legs will be on the same thread. Start with 1 of the ¼-inch round beads, then add a red circle, a small wooden bead, a white circle, a small wooden bead, etc. Use 7 circles of each color felt and end with a white circle. This will be the top of the first leg. Continue down the other leg, beginning with a white circle. Alternate 7 circles of each color, placing a small bead between each felt circle. End with a red circle and a ¼-inch round bead. Pull the thread taut and tie a knot securely.

Body—Attach the thread to the center of the leg area at the point where the 2 white circles are together. Starting with a white circle, alternate 5 circles of each color, placing a small bead between each circle. End with a red circle and leave a long piece of thread.

Arms—Both arms will be on the same thread. Using a new thread, start with a ¼-inch round bead, then alternate 6 circles of each color beginning with a red one. Put a small bead between each circle and

end at the center with a white piece. Continue down the other arm, starting with a white circle and alternating colors and beads. End with a red circle and a ¼-inch round bead. Pull the thread tight and knot it.

Neck—Join the arms to the body by tightly knotting the long body thread to the center of the arms (2 white circles together). To make the neck, use a white circle, a small bead, and a red circle.

Head—Join the head to the body by drawing the thread through the hole in the 1-inch bead and then through the small flat bead. Knot tightly and leave an end for a hanger.

Hair—Glue 2-inch pieces of yellow yarn hair on the bead.

Face—With a fine brush paint on a red mouth. When dry, use a fine pointed indelible black felt pen to draw eyes and the center mouth line.

NOTE: A hat of red felt may be added.

Contributed by Mrs. Neal Wood
St. Louis, Missouri

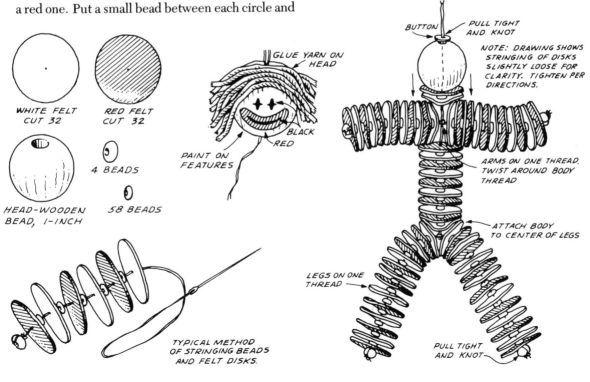

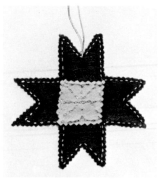

FEATHER STAR

Colored felt (2 8-inch x 9-inch pieces in different colors will make 1 star)
Pencil
Pinking shears
Colored embroidery thread

Embroidery needle
Fiberfill, cotton batting, or shredded nylon stockings

Trace the pattern onto the felt. Cut 1 star and 1 square from each color with the pinking shears. Sew the 2 stars together. Stitch around the outside edges with embroidery thread, leaving 1 point open. Stuff lightly and sew opening closed. Place a square of contrasting color on the star as shown. Stitch around the edges of the square and sew diagonally across the square from 1 corner to the other to form an X. Repeat with the other square on the opposite side. Attach a loop of thread for a hanger.

HISTORY: This feather star design is a contemporary variation on an old patchwork quilt pattern.

Contributed by Mrs. Judith W. Blood
Far Hills, New Jersey

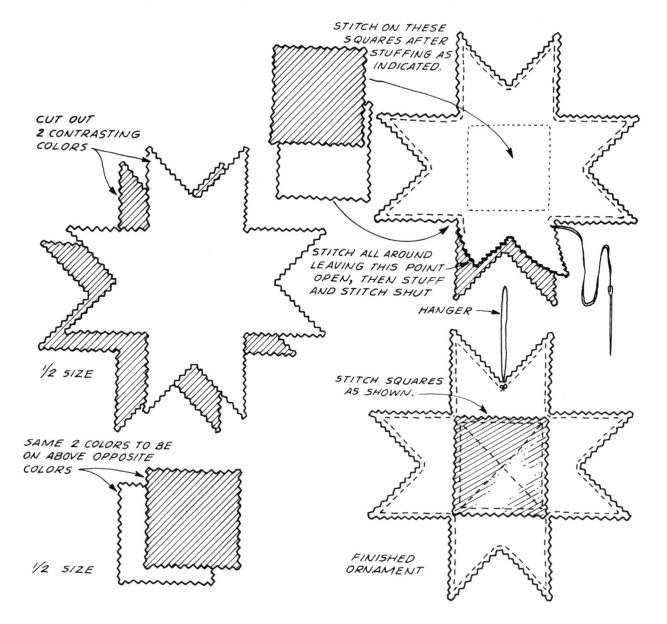

STITCH ON THESE SQUARES AFTER STUFFING AS INDICATED.

CUT OUT 2 CONTRASTING COLORS

STITCH ALL AROUND LEAVING THIS POINT OPEN, THEN STUFF AND STITCH SHUT

HANGER

1/2 SIZE

SAME 2 COLORS TO BE ON ABOVE OPPOSITE COLORS

STITCH SQUARES AS SHOWN.

1/2 SIZE

FINISHED ORNAMENT

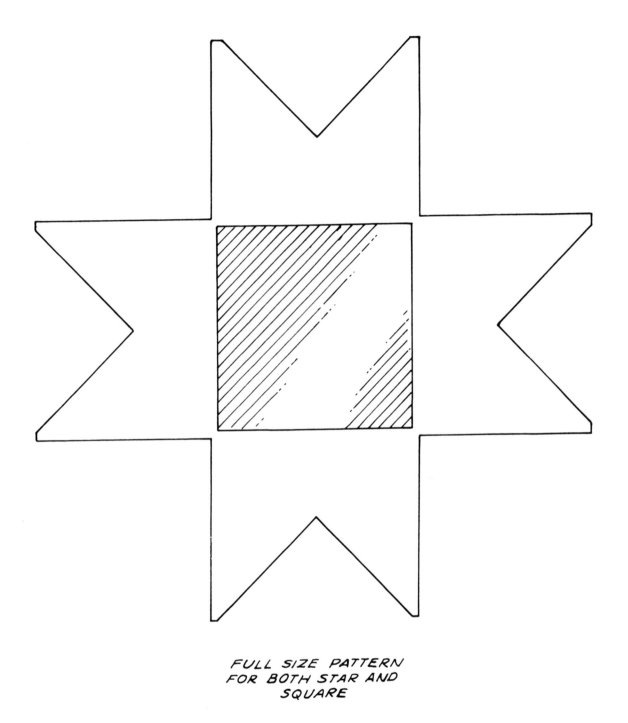

FULL SIZE PATTERN
FOR BOTH STAR AND
SQUARE

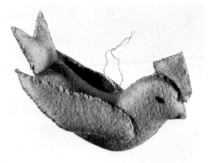

BIRD

Colored felt (1 8-inch x 9-inch
   piece makes 1 bird)
Pencil
Scissors
Sewing needle

Matching thread
Fiberfill, cotton batting, or shredded
   nylon stockings
Bead

Trace the following pattern pieces onto the felt and cut out:

Tail—A 2 pieces
Body—B 2 pieces
Wing—C 4 pieces
Crest—D 2 pieces

Leaving the tail open, overcast all around the body and stuff firmly with fiberfill, cotton batting, or shredded nylon stockings. Sew the tail end closed as shown. Overcast the wings, crest, and tail leaving 1 end open for stuffing; stuff lightly and sew closed. Placing seam to seam, sew the crest and tail into place. Attach the wings to the body. Sew on a bead for an eye, or make one with black thread. Make a hanger of yarn or thread.

Contributed by Mrs. Beulah Rogers
Williamsburg, Virginia

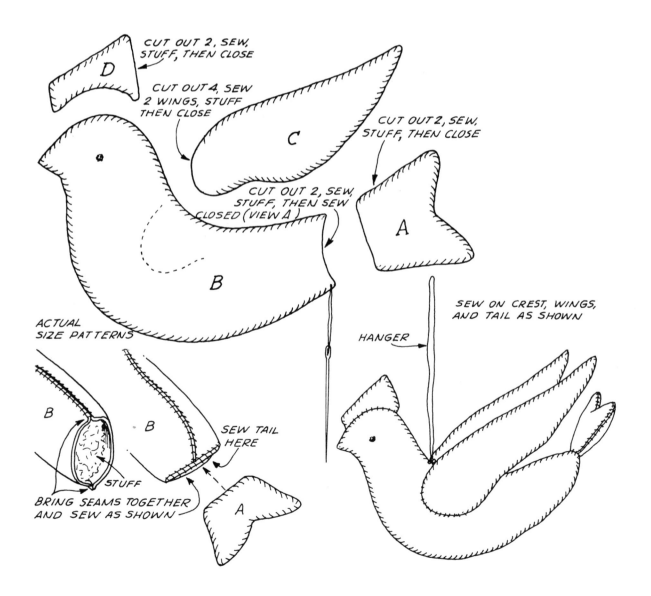

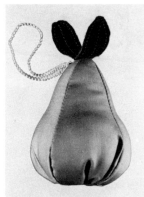

PEAR

Pencil
Gingham or calico-type fabric
Scissors
Sewing needle

Matching thread
Fiberfill, cotton batting, or shredded
    nylon stockings
Scraps of green felt

Trace the pear pattern onto the fabric and cut out 4 sections. Starting and ending at the dots, stitch the pieces together on the wrong side of the fabric leaving a ¼-inch seam. The top of the pear will be almost closed, the bottom open. Clip the curves and turn the pear right side out. Gather around the bottom opening, pull closed, and fasten off the thread. Turn the edges on the circle of fabric under and sew it over the bottom. Cut 2 leaves from green felt. Sew a row of stitches down the center of each and gather stitching slightly to give a leaflike appearance. Attach the leaves to the top of the pear.

Contributed by Mrs. Eflyn B. Morris
Williamsburg, Virginia

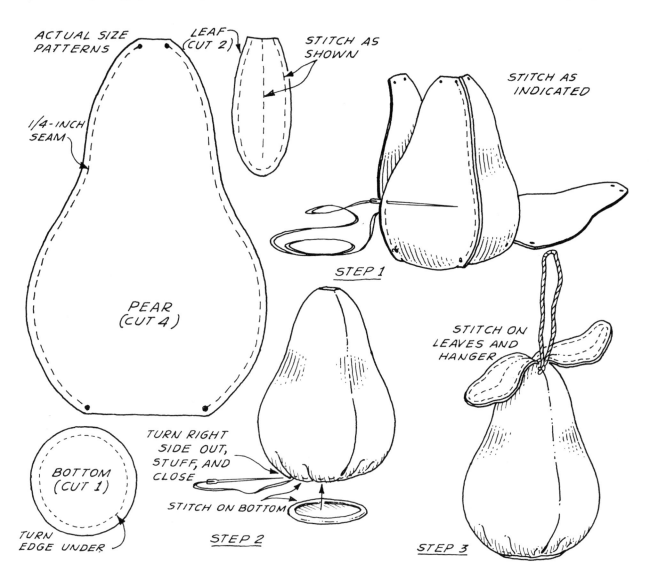

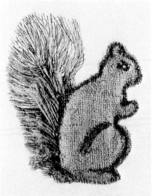

BURLAP ANIMALS

Natural color burlap
Matching thread
Pencil
Straight pins
Scissors
Sewing machine
Fiberfill, cotton batting, or shredded
 nylon stockings
Long pin or stiff brush for fringing
Felt tipped pens or paints in assorted
 colors for marking features

Crochet hook
White glue
Scraps of white felt
White thread
Sewing needle
Small stick (for owl's perch)
Small feathers (for owl)
Broom straws (for whiskers)
Calico scrap (for horse's saddle)

All animals—Double the burlap, pin the two pieces together, and trace the pattern onto the fabric. Burlap frays easily, so work carefully. Set the sewing machine on the shortest stitch before cutting out the pattern. Sew on the dotted lines, including inside areas such as the squirrel's and cat's tails, and the horse's mane. Leave a 1-inch opening where indicated for stuffing. Cut out on the solid lines. Stuff lightly, working with small pieces of stuffing. Sew up the opening on the machine. Carefully fringe all around.

Owl—Sew ⅛ inch from the edge of the 2 eye circles and fringe. Place a small circle of white felt on each of the burlap eye circles and sew them to the owl with the white thread, overlapping the circles slightly as shown. Ink or paint on black eyes,

beak, wings, and feet. Push a small twig through the owl's claws.

Horse—Fringe the mane and tail. Cut a saddle from a scrap of calico and glue it over the back of the horse. Ink or paint on features.

Squirrel—The blunt end of a crochet hook is handy for pushing tiny pieces of stuffing into its tail. Carefully cut along the solid line down the squirrel's back to the dot as indicated and fringe. A stiff brush helps to make the tail look bushy. Brush upward. For whiskers, poke broomstraws through the burlap. Draw on an eye and any other features desired.

Cat—See the squirrel.

Contributed by Mrs. Anne Warlow
Reston, Virginia

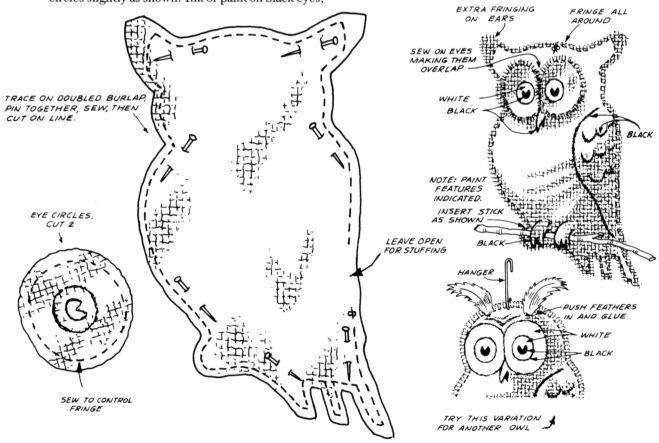

THESE PATTERNS ARE ACTUAL SIZE

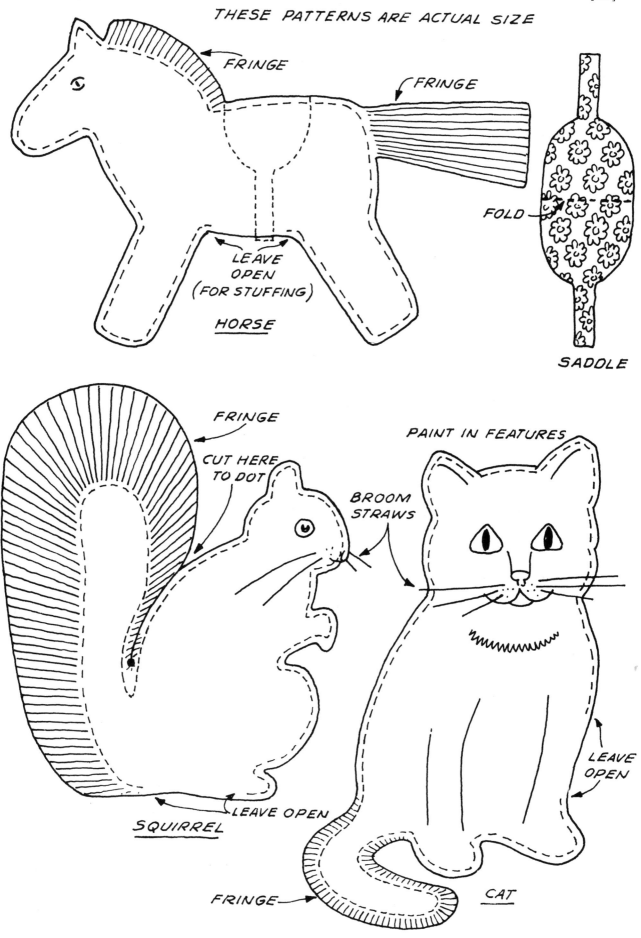

FRINGE

FRINGE

LEAVE
OPEN
(FOR STUFFING)

HORSE

FOLD

SADOLE

FRINGE

CUT HERE
TO DOT

PAINT IN FEATURES

BROOM
STRAWS

LEAVE OPEN

SQUIRREL

LEAVE
OPEN

FRINGE

CAT

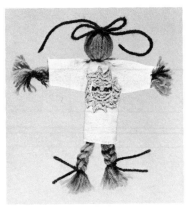

YARN DOLL

Worsted woolen yarn (assorted primary or earth colors)
Scissors
Cotton ball

Cotton fabric for dress
Thread
Sewing needle

Cut 28 pieces of worsted or other fairly heavy yarn 24 inches long. Place the strands of yarn neatly side by side to form a bunch. Double the yarn, tie it in the center, leaving the ends of the tie for a hanger, and tie a bow around the strands about 1 inch below the fold to form the doll's head. Insert a cotton ball and pull the yarn over it so that it is covered. Divide the yarn below the head into 4 separate sections with 14 strands in each section. Two of these will be used to make the arms, and the other 2 strands will form the legs. Braid 2 of the sections until they are about 5 inches long. Tie the end of each braid with yarn and cut off any excess. These are the doll's arms and hands.

Make the body by tying the remaining 2 sections together with yarn about 3 inches below the arms. Then either braid them or just tie them together at each end to form legs. Left loose, the yarn will look like a skirt. Trim any ragged edges.

Details may be added by using different colors of yarn to tie the sections together, by adding fabric eyes and mouth to the face, or by sewing a simple cotton dress.

This doll has many variations. The proportions of the strands may be changed to suit the maker. The finished doll will be approximately ½ of the length of the original strand.

Contributed by Ms. Ann Brown
Williamsburg, Virginia

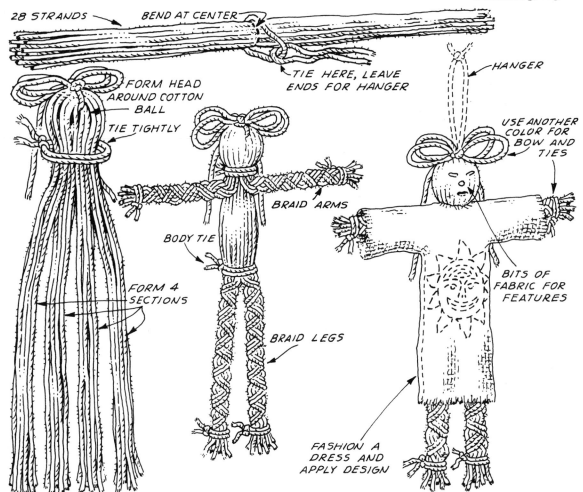

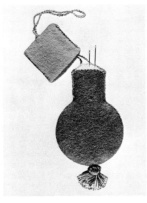

KOREAN NEEDLE CASE

Thin cardboard
Scissors
White glue
Green and red felt
Green and red sewing thread

Sewing needle
Green and red buttonhole twist
  thread
Small crochet hook
Cotton balls or human hair

Using the pattern, cut the case and top out of thin cardboard. Glue the cardboard case to the green felt and the cardboard top to the red felt. Allow to dry. Trim away excess felt, leaving about 1/16 inch around the edge for stitching the case and top. Stitch the case with the cardboard sides toward the inside, leaving the top open. Decorate around the seam with a chain stitch using red buttonhole twist thread. Stitch the side seams of the top and decorate with chain stitch using green buttonhole twist. The top should slip over the top of the case easily.

Crochet a chain about 10 inches long with red buttonhold twist thread and attach it to the case on each side as shown. Cut a small hole in the center of the top, being sure to pierce both the felt and the cardboard. Thread the chain through the center of the top. Knot the chain to keep the top from slipping off.

Make a tassel of buttonhole twist thread by cutting many 2-inch pieces of thread. The thickness depends on the number of pieces used. Multicolored threads look very nice. Tie several pieces of thread around the middle of the bundle of threads. Fold in half. Tie double threads around the bunch 1/4 inch down from the top. Tie very tightly so that the threads are not loose and cannot be pulled out. Using red buttonhole twist thread, sew the tassel to the bottom of the case.

Stuff the case lightly with hair or cotton balls. Insert extra sewing needles into the stuffing.

HISTORY: Korean women use these cases to store their sewing needles and often attach the cases to their belts. Needles are precious, and great care is used to preserve them. Human hair is considered the best stuffing because oil on the hair keeps the needles from rusting.

Contributed by Mrs. Kyu Hargrave
Williamsburg, Virginia

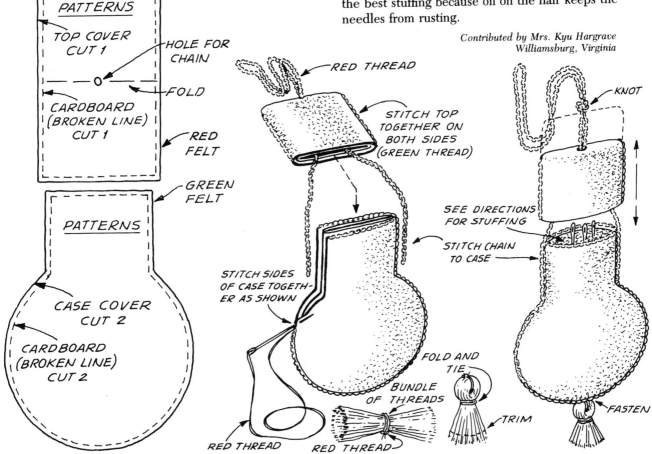

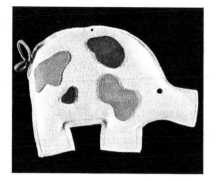

COOKIE CUTTER STUFFED ORNAMENT

Cookie cutter or pattern shown
  below
Pencil
Fabric—cotton, calico, felt, wool,
  suede cloth, leather
Straight pins
Scissors or pinking shears

Sewing needle
Colored thread
Fiberfill, cotton batting, or
  shredded nylon stockings
Colored yarn, buttons, or any
  other trim desired

Make a pattern by tracing a cookie cutter directly onto the fabric, trace a pattern from this book, or draw a figure of your own. Pin the pattern onto a double layer of fabric. If the material will be sewn on the wrong side and turned right side out, add an additional ¼ inch to the pattern. With scissors or pinking shears, cut out the 2 layers of fabric along these lines.

METHOD I: Sew the right sides together ¼ inch from the edge. Leave a 1-inch space to insert the stuffing. Trim seam edges, turn right side out, and stuff with fiberfill, stockings, or other lightweight filler. Stitch up the stuffing hole. Add eyes (buttons may be used), tail, wings, or mane using scraps of fabric or yarn. Sew on a thread loop for hanging the ornament.

METHOD II: With the right sides of the fabric facing outward, stitch together ¼ inch from the edge. Leave a 1-inch space for stuffing. Stuff with fiberfill, shredded stockings, or lightweight filler. Sew up the stuffing hole. Add eyes and other decorations and a thread loop for hanging. This is a faster method; however, *pinking shears should be used* in cutting out the fabric because these edges are exposed and may fray unless pinked.

Contributed by Mrs. Judith W. Blood
Far Hills, New Jersey

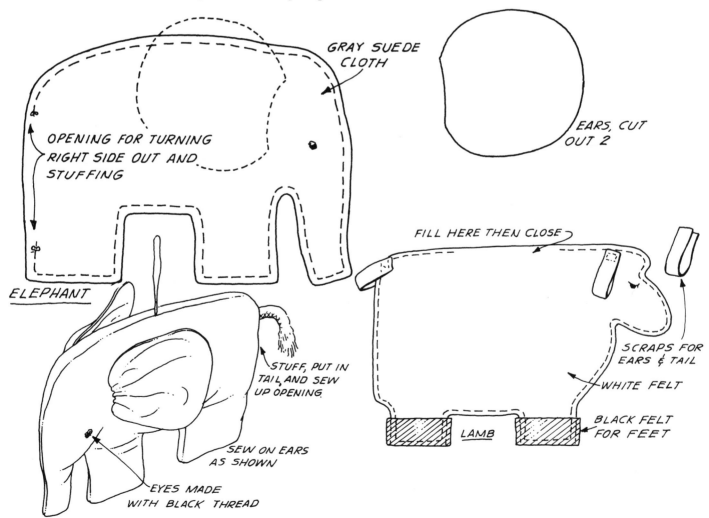

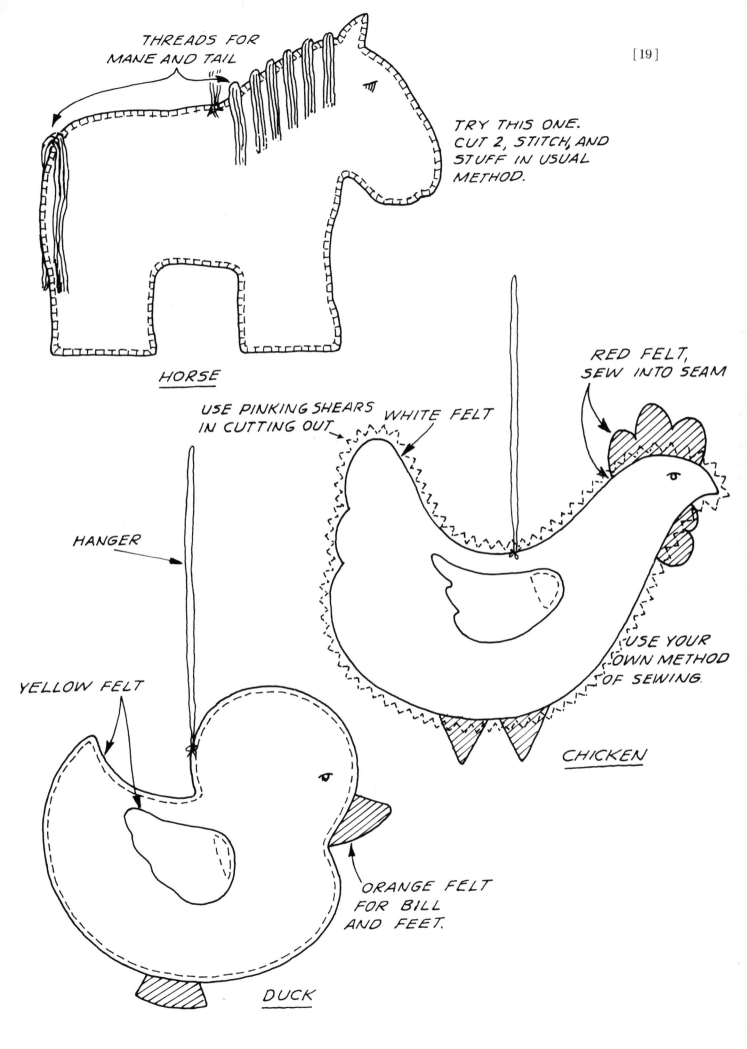

THREADS FOR MANE AND TAIL

TRY THIS ONE. CUT 2, STITCH, AND STUFF IN USUAL METHOD.

HORSE

USE PINKING SHEARS IN CUTTING OUT

WHITE FELT

RED FELT, SEW INTO SEAM

HANGER

USE YOUR OWN METHOD OF SEWING.

CHICKEN

YELLOW FELT

ORANGE FELT FOR BILL AND FEET.

DUCK

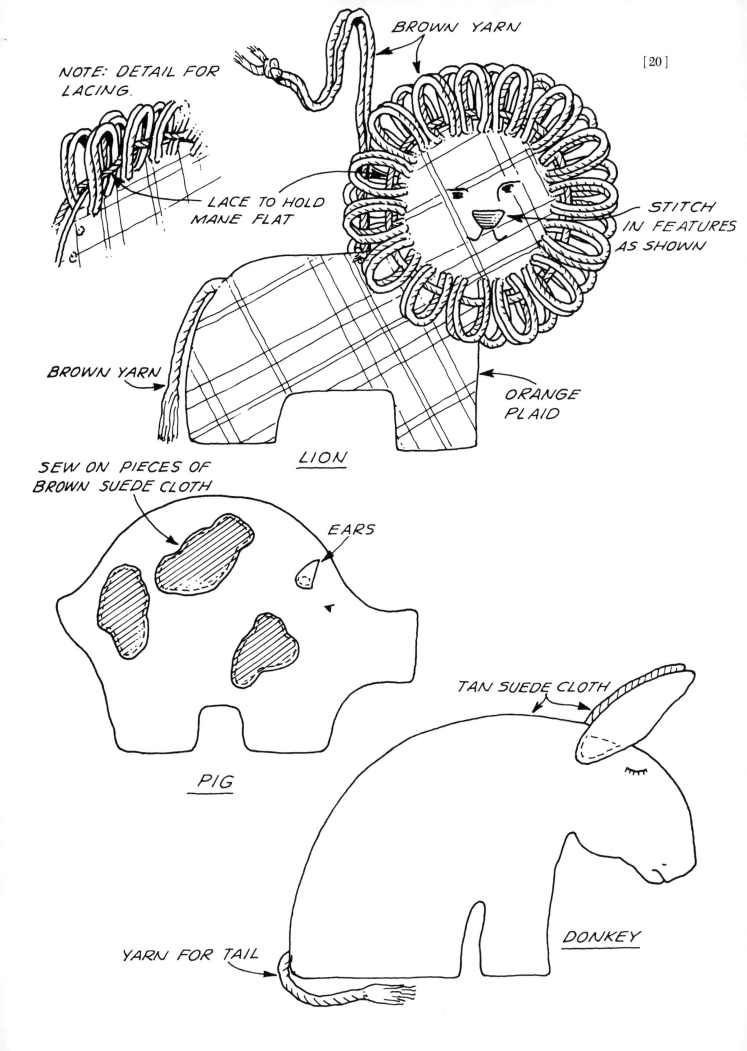

NOTE: DETAIL FOR LACING.

BROWN YARN

LACE TO HOLD MANE FLAT

STITCH IN FEATURES AS SHOWN

BROWN YARN

ORANGE PLAID

LION

SEW ON PIECES OF BROWN SUEDE CLOTH

EARS

PIG

TAN SUEDE CLOTH

DONKEY

YARN FOR TAIL

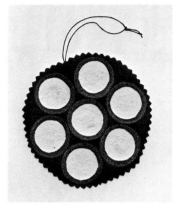

PENNY RUG DESIGNS

Colored felt—1 square black,
   1 square white, approximately 8 x 8
   inches
Pinking shears
Scraps of colored felt

1 penny, 1 quarter
Scissors
White glue
Sewing needle
Black thread

Using the pinking shears, cut 3-inch circles in white or black felt. With the scissors cut several small felt circles in contrasting colors the size of a penny and a quarter. Glue quarter-size circles onto a large white or black felt circle in a design of your choice. Glue penny-size circles of different colors of felt onto the quarter-size circles. Decorate both sides. Concentric circles that vary in size and color can also be glued onto the large black or white circles. Sew on a loop of thread for a hanger.

Contributed by Ms. Cathy Gibbons
Williamsburg, Virginia

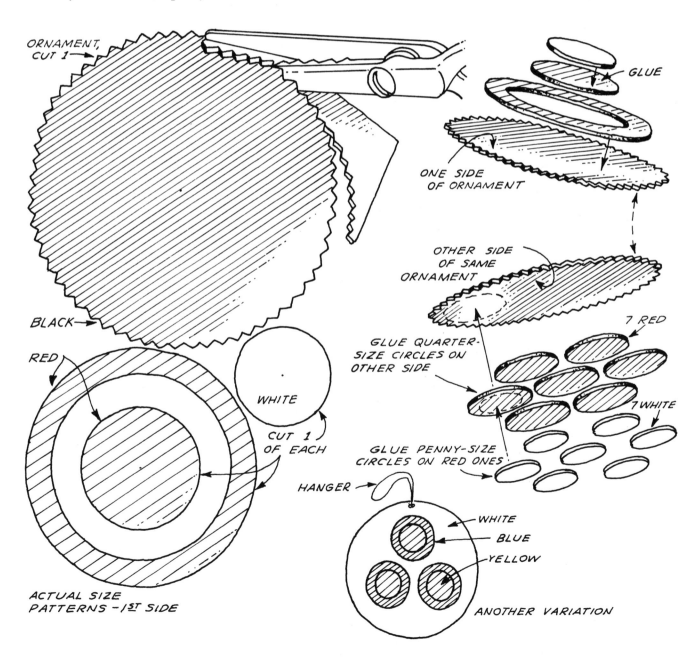

ORNAMENT, CUT 1

GLUE

ONE SIDE OF ORNAMENT

OTHER SIDE OF SAME ORNAMENT

7 RED

GLUE QUARTER-SIZE CIRCLES ON OTHER SIDE

7 WHITE

BLACK

RED

WHITE

CUT 1 OF EACH

GLUE PENNY-SIZE CIRCLES ON RED ONES

HANGER

WHITE

BLUE

YELLOW

ACTUAL SIZE PATTERNS - 1ST SIDE

ANOTHER VARIATION

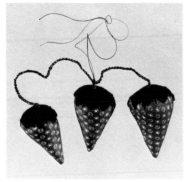

STRAWBERRY

Red and white checked or
  polka-dotted fabric
Pencil
Scissors
Sewing needle
White and green thread

Fiberfill, cotton batting, or shredded
  nylon stockings
Green felt
Small crochet hook
Green embroidery or buttonhole
  thread

Trace the pattern onto the red and white checked or polka-dotted fabric and cut out. Stitch together on the wrong side of the fabric, leaving an opening at the rounded edge. Turn to the right side and run a row of stitching around the curved edge. Stuff, then pull this stitching up tightly. Cut a top from green felt and attach it to the top of the berry with green thread. Use a chain stitch to crochet stems from green embroidery or buttonhole thread.

Contributed by Mrs. Doris Epps
Williamsburg, Virginia

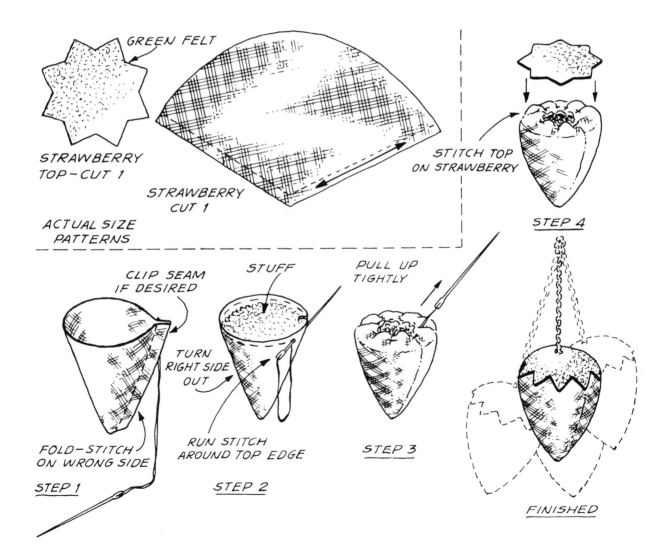

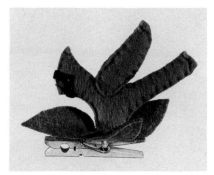

CLOTHESPIN CARDINAL

Red felt (1 8-inch x 9-inch piece will make 2 birds)
Pencil
Scissors
Straight pins
Sewing needle
Thread

Fiberfill, cotton batting, or shredded nylon stockings
Black felt
Small black beads
Green felt
White glue
3-inch pinch clothespin

Trace the bird pattern onto the red felt with a pencil. Cut out the felt pieces. Sew around the edges of the cardinal's body, leaving a 1-inch space open at the bottom. Stuff the bird with cotton or fiberfill. Sew the red felt base onto the bottom of the bird. Sew the 2 wing pieces together, leaving a 1-inch opening at the round end, and stuff. Open the ends over either side of the body and stitch. Cut out 2 small pieces of black felt, sew them together at their ends as shown, then sew onto the cardinal's face. For eyes, attach small black beads. Trace the leaf pattern onto the green felt and cut out 3. Glue the leaves to the top of a 3-inch pinch clothespin, covering the wood, then glue or sew the stuffed bird onto the leaves. Attach the clothespin to the tree.

Contributed by Miss Jane Blunn
Chicago, Illinois

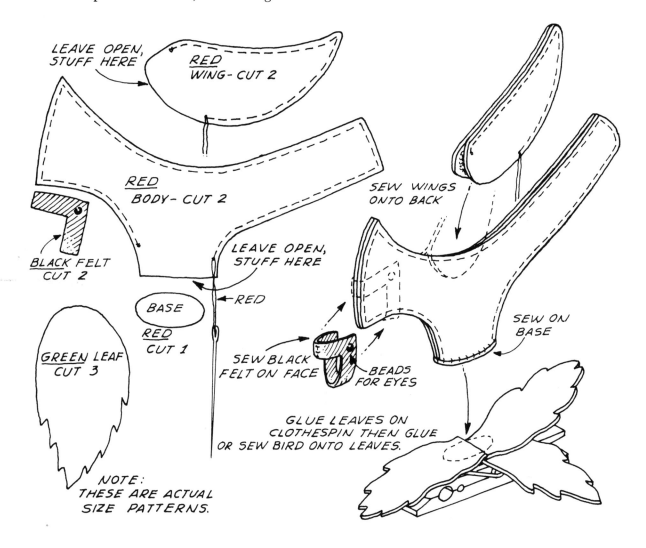

LEAVE OPEN, STUFF HERE

RED
WING- CUT 2

RED
BODY- CUT 2

BLACK FELT
CUT 2

LEAVE OPEN,
STUFF HERE

←RED

BASE
RED
CUT 1

GREEN LEAF
CUT 3

SEW BLACK
FELT ON FACE

BEADS
FOR EYES

NOTE:
THESE ARE ACTUAL
SIZE PATTERNS.

SEW WINGS
ONTO BACK

SEW ON
BASE

GLUE LEAVES ON
CLOTHESPIN THEN GLUE
OR SEW BIRD ONTO LEAVES.

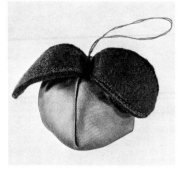

APPLE

Pencil
Red fabric
Green felt
Scissors
Red thread
Sewing needle

Fiberfill, cotton batting, or shredded
   nylon stockings
Long needle with a large eye
Green yarn, 12 inches long
Green thread

Trace the patterns onto the fabrics and cut out. For the apple, stitch seams on the wrong side of the fabric sewing A to A, B to B, C to C, and D to D with a ¼-inch seam. Leave the top open. Clip the curved seams and turn right side out. Stitch around the top with a running stitch. Stuff. Pull thread to close the opening. Fasten off the thread. Thread the yarn through a long needle and make a large knot at the end. Invert the needle at the bottom and come up through the closure stitching. Pull the yarn tight and knot, leaving the end for a hanger. To make each leaf, stitch 2 pieces together and gather to form a natural crease. Sew the leaves onto the apple over the top closure stitching.

Contributed by Mrs. Eleanor Hutson
Williamsburg, Virginia

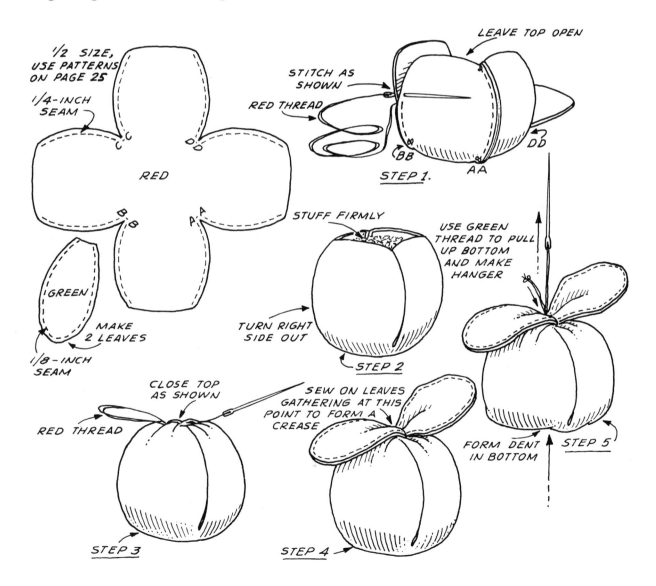

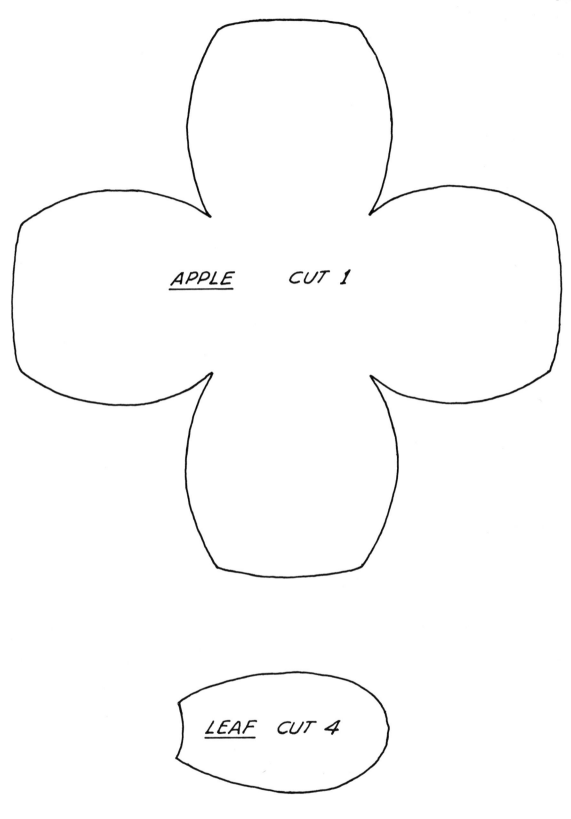

APPLE   CUT 1

LEAF   CUT 4

ACTUAL SIZE

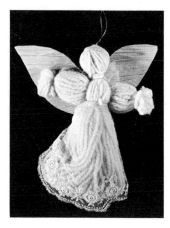

CORNHUSK, YARN, AND LACE ANGEL

Cream colored knitting yarn
1 piece of cardboard 5½ inches x 5
   inches
Scissors
Tissue paper

Sewing needle
Cream colored thread
Cream colored lace, netting, or
   chiffon scraps (for skirt and halo)
1 cornhusk at least 6 inches long

Wrap yarn around the 5½-inch side of the cardboard 50 times to obtain the right length for the body; remove yarn and tie a short length of yarn close to 1 end. This makes a small neck. (The head will be added later.) Wrap another length of yarn around the 5-inch side of the cardboard 35 times to form the arms. Tie a short length of yarn around ¾ inch from each end to make the hands.

Put the shorter length through the longer length up at the neck; then tie a short piece of yarn around the body below the arms to form the waist and also to hold the arms in position.

To form the head, wad a small amount of tissue paper into a marble-size ball, then wrap firmly with yarn. Sew this onto the neck. Leave 2 strands of yarn at the top of the head to make a hanger.

Cut a piece of lace or material for a skirt and sew into position. Sew on another narrow piece for a halo. Cut wings out of 1 piece of cornhusk and sew the middle of the husk to the middle of the angel's back. If you use husks that have not been dried previously, place the wings between newspapers, weight them down with a book, and dry completely (about 5 days).

Contributed by Mrs. Ellen Jones
St. Louis, Missouri

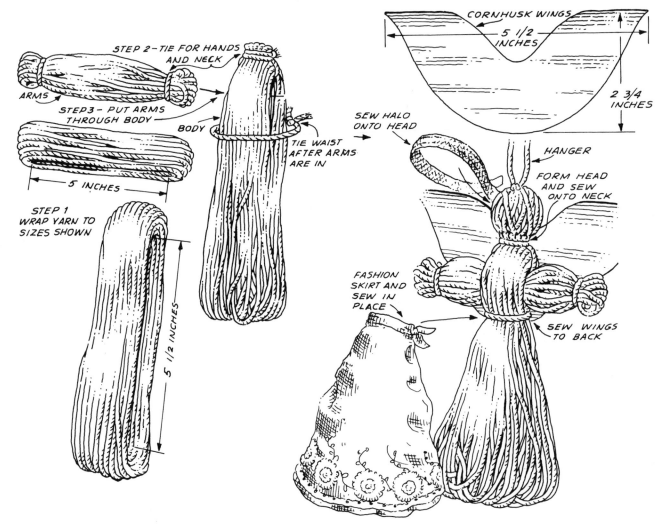

SAND DOLLAR AND STARFISH

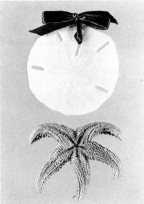

Dried starfish (can be purchased at
    any ocean resort)
Scissors
Lightweight clear plastic fishing line

Wrap thin lightweight fishing line around the
starfish as a hanger. Tie securely and hang.

Contributed by Mrs. Charles E. Thwaite III
Atlanta, Georgia

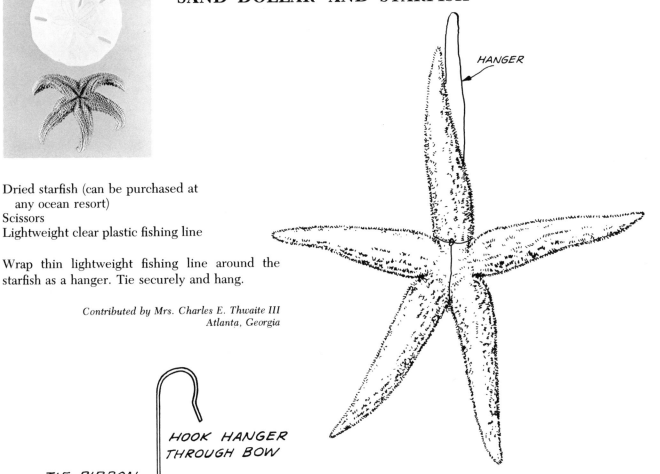

HANGER

HOOK HANGER
THROUGH BOW

TIE RIBBON
AS SHOWN

ACTUAL SIZE

Sand dollars
Bleach
Red or green satin ribbon, ¼ inch
    wide
Christmas tree hanger

Collect sand dollars on the beach and dry
thoroughly. Soak the sand dollars in a strong bleach
solution (3 parts bleach to 1 part water) for a day or
until they are white. Rinse thoroughly with water
and dry in the sun. Sand dollars are extremely
fragile and must be handled with great care. When
completely dry, tie a satin bow through the long
center hole in the sand dollar. Attach a tree hanger
to the bow.

Contributed by Mrs. Charles E. Thwaite III
Atlanta, Georgia

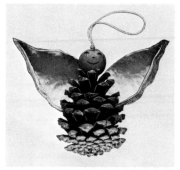

PINECONE ANGEL

Heavy scissors or flower clippers
3-inch pine cone
2 dried milkweed pods (gather them in the fall)
White glue

Black felt pen with a fine point
Hickory nut, small walnut, or other nut about 1¼ inches high
Small piece of string or yarn for hanger

Cut off the top bracts (petals) from the pinecone to make room for the angel's head, which is the nut. Take the milkweed pods, hollow side facing out, and push into the back of the cone to form wings. Glue and let dry.

Make facial features on the nut head with the black felt pen, then glue it onto the cone. When dry, glue on a hanger of string or yarn.

Contributed by Pompey Hollow Peaches 4-H Club
Manlius, New York

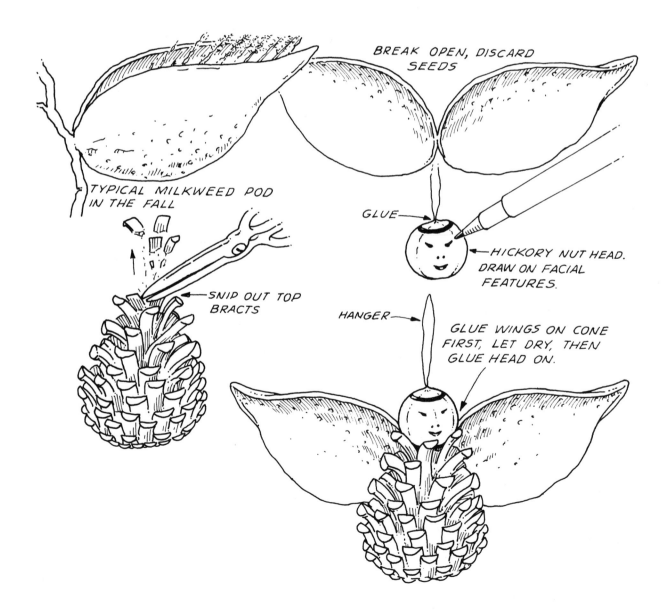

BREAK OPEN, DISCARD SEEDS

TYPICAL MILKWEED POD IN THE FALL

SNIP OUT TOP BRACTS

GLUE

HICKORY NUT HEAD. DRAW ON FACIAL FEATURES.

HANGER

GLUE WINGS ON CONE FIRST, LET DRY, THEN GLUE HEAD ON.

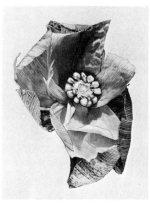

CORNHUSK FLOWER

Field corn with shucks attached
Knife or cleaver
Scissors
Boiling water

Tea kettle or large pan
Optional—darning or tapestry
   needle

Gather field corn in the fall after the first frost has turned the ears of corn down. Be careful to leave 2 to 3 inches of stem. Pull back the husks, exposing the entire ear. Using a knife or cleaver, cut away all but the last ½ inch of the ear, leaving approximately 3 rows of kernels, which will be used for the center of the flower. Returning the husks to their original position, cut each of them with the scissors to resemble petals.

With water boiling in a kettle, work over it shaping each petal with your hands. The steam makes the petals very pliable. The longer the husks are, the larger the flowers will be.

A variation is to use a darning or tapestry needle to shred each petal and form a chrysanthemum-like flower. No two flowers will be alike.

Contributed by Mrs. Frances Stratton
Cazenovia, New York

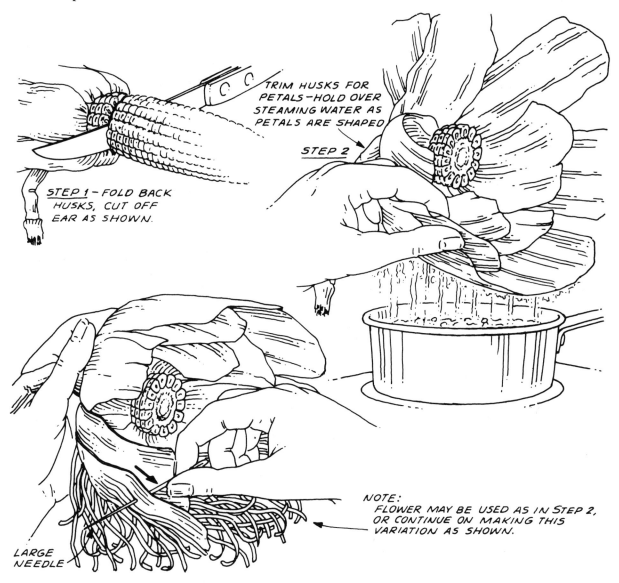

TRIM HUSKS FOR PETALS—HOLD OVER STEAMING WATER AS PETALS ARE SHAPED

STEP 2

STEP 1—FOLD BACK HUSKS, CUT OFF EAR AS SHOWN.

LARGE NEEDLE

NOTE:
FLOWER MAY BE USED AS IN STEP 2, OR CONTINUE ON MAKING THIS VARIATION AS SHOWN.

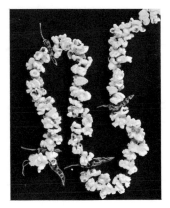

POPCORN AND RED PEPPER STRING

Sturdy white thread
Long sharp sewing needle
Dried red peppers, 1 to 2 inches long
Freshly popped white popcorn,
    unsalted and unbuttered—one
    large bowl makes a 5-foot chain

Thread the needle and put it through 1 red pepper either lengthwise or widthwise. Tie the thread securely around the pepper to form a knot. Thread the popcorn onto the string alternating peppers and popcorn. You can use 1 pepper to every 6 to 12 pieces of popcorn or alternate popcorn and peppers.

Make the chain as long as you like. However, if it is over 6 feet long, the chain becomes difficult to handle. Several chains can be tied together before putting them on the tree.

Only freshly popped corn should be used because stale popcorn tends to shatter.

Contributed by Ms. Ann Brown
Williamsburg, Virginia

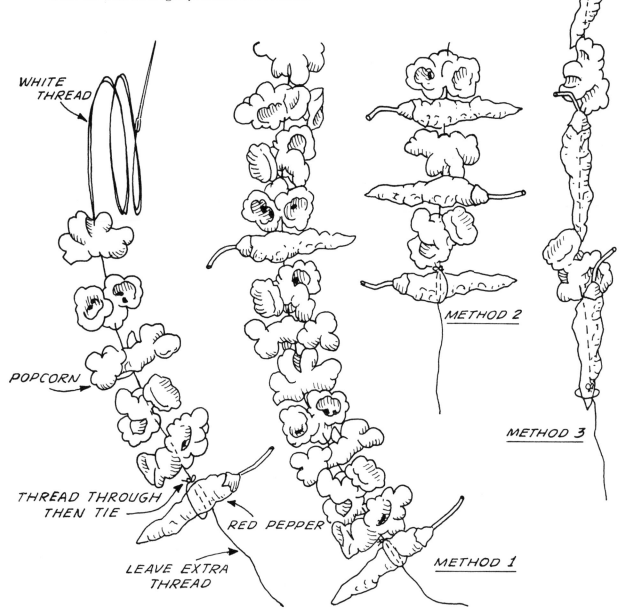

WHITE THREAD

POPCORN

THREAD THROUGH THEN TIE

RED PEPPER

LEAVE EXTRA THREAD

METHOD 1

METHOD 2

METHOD 3

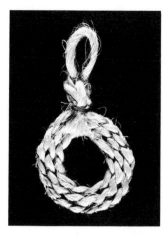

BALING TWINE WREATH

Baling twine, baler twine doubled,
    heavy macramé cord, or other
    heavy twine
Scissors
Large pointed sewing needle
6-strand red and green embroidery
    thread

Tie a loop 1½ inches in diameter at 1 end of a 90-inch-long piece of baling twine or cord. Cut the remainder of the long strand into 3 sections and join them as shown, then braid tightly until all the twine is used. Roll the braid into a circle so that the braid is flat against itself. Leave a hole in the center. Thread the needle with 2 24-inch-long strands of embroidery thread, 1 red and 1 green, and sew the braids together. Work up and down around the circle as shown, making each stitch at least ¼ inch

long so that it shows clearly as you sew the braids together. Stitch down the loose end of the knot of the loop, which is the hanger. This amount of heavy baling twine will make a 3-row circle about 3 inches in diameter.

NOTE: Different colors, textures, weights, and lengths of materials will create variations.

Contributed by Mrs. Alice Mapes
Manlius, New York

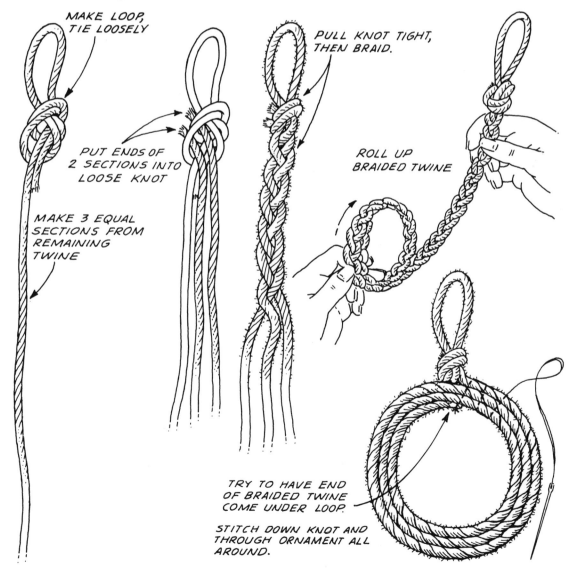

MAKE LOOP,
TIE LOOSELY

PUT ENDS OF
2 SECTIONS INTO
LOOSE KNOT

MAKE 3 EQUAL
SECTIONS FROM
REMAINING
TWINE

PULL KNOT TIGHT,
THEN BRAID.

ROLL UP
BRAIDED TWINE

TRY TO HAVE END
OF BRAIDED TWINE
COME UNDER LOOP.

STITCH DOWN KNOT AND
THROUGH ORNAMENT ALL
AROUND.

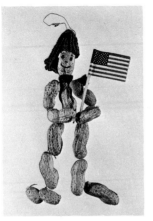

YANKEE-DOODLE PEANUT MAN

Long pointed needle
Fine cloth-covered wire or similar fine pliable wire on a spool or lightweight clear plastic fishing line
12 dried and unsalted peanuts in their shells (use the largest shell for the body)

Black felt tipped marking pen
Sock ribbing
White glue
Scissors
Sewing needle
Thread
Paper flag on a toothpick

Starting at 1 foot, thread the wire or fishing line through a peanut shell widthwise, thread on 2 peanut shells lengthwise, then thread through the extreme end of the peanut shell body. Continue through 2 peanut shells lengthwise and another small shell widthwise. This makes 2 legs attached to the body. Make a little twist at the end of each wire so that the peanut shells cannot slip off, or tie a knot in the fishing line.

Thread 2 peanut shells on the wire lengthwise, pass the wire through the body peanut shell at about shoulder height, and add 2 more peanuts threaded lengthwise. This makes the arms. Twist the wire ends of the arms together or tie off. Add a head by wiring the end of another peanut shell to the tip of the body peanut. Make features on the lower half of the head with a black felt tipped marking pen.

With right sides together, seam a small piece of sock ribbing, turn it right side out, and glue it to the top half of the peanut head so that it tilts over the side of the head. You can add a scarf made from a strip of sock ribbing 3 inches long and ¾ inches wide. Attach a hanging wire or thread to the top of the head. Insert a paper flag on a toothpick in one hand.

Contributed by Mrs. William Galloway
Hampton, Virginia

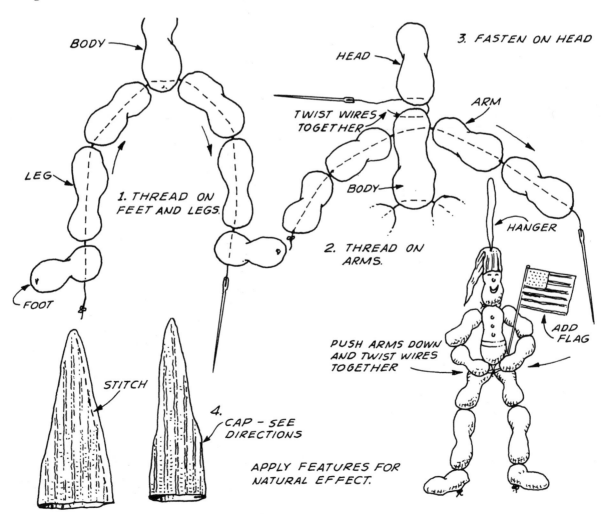

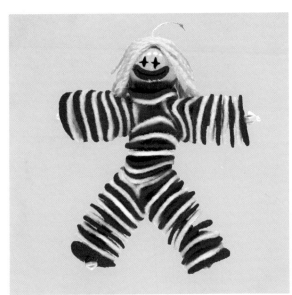

FELT CLOWN, *page 9*

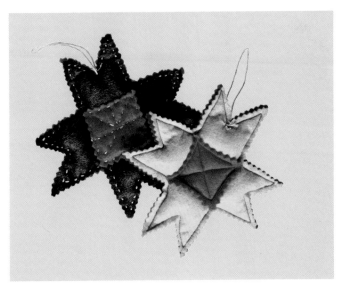

FEATHER STAR, *page 10*

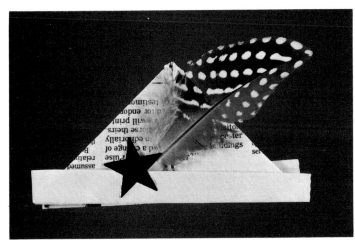

NEWSPAPER SOLDIER HAT, *page 55*

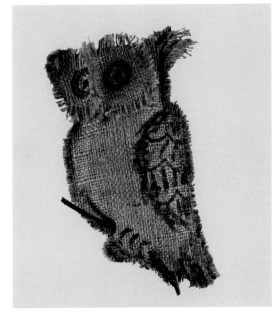

BURLAP ANIMAL, *page 14*

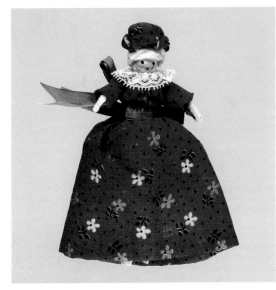

CLOTHESPIN DOLL, *page 76*

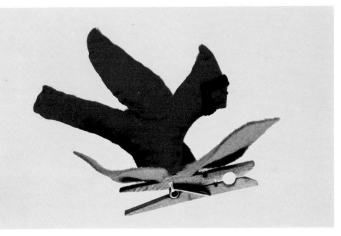

CLOTHESPIN CARDINAL, *page 23*

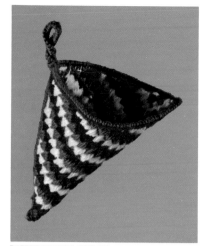
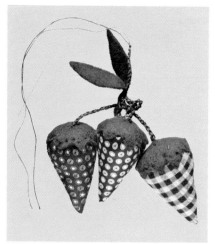
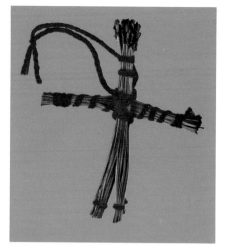

**NEEDLEPOINT
CORNUCOPIA,** *page 53*

STRAWBERRY, *page 22*

PINE NEEDLE MAN, *page 41*

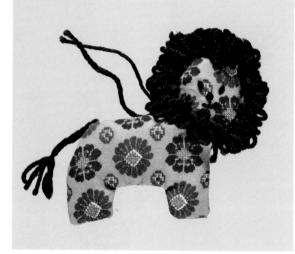
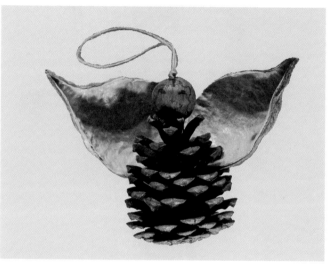

COOKIE CUTTER STUFFED ORNAMENT,
page 18

PINECONE ANGEL, *page 28*

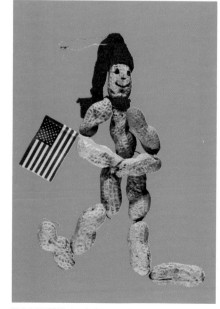
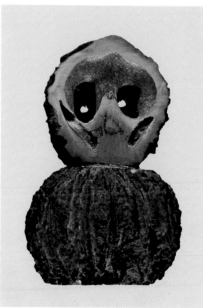
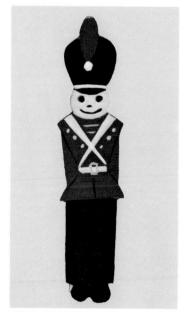

**YANKEE-DOODLE
PEANUT MAN,** *page 32*

BLACK WALNUT OWL, *page 36*

CLOTHESPIN SOLDIER,
page 69

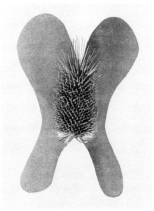

TEASEL BUTTERFLY

Colored or decorated paper
Pencil
Scissors
White glue
Teasel

Fold the paper and trace the pattern onto it. Cut out 2 sets of wings. Glue them together right side out. Crease along folding lines, then apply glue inside the crease and press together. Glue the mid-section and push it into the burr. Let it dry overnight. Carefully spread the wings. No string or hook is needed; the burr will easily sit on a tree limb.

A teasel is a small burr commonly found growing along the roadside. It once was used to raise the nap on woolen cloth.

Contributed by Ms. Bryding Adams
Williamsburg, Virginia

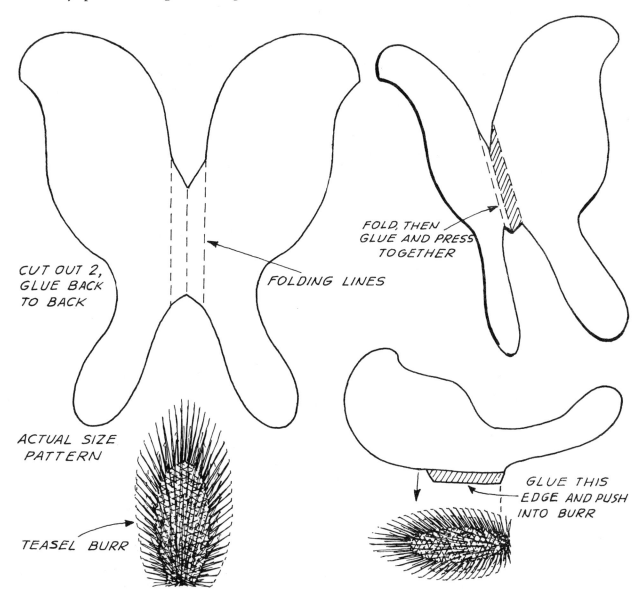

CUT OUT 2, GLUE BACK TO BACK

FOLDING LINES

ACTUAL SIZE PATTERN

TEASEL BURR

FOLD, THEN GLUE AND PRESS TOGETHER

GLUE THIS EDGE AND PUSH INTO BURR

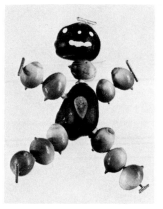

NUT PEOPLE

Nuts, acorns, buckeyes (horse chestnuts), walnuts
Hemlock and pinecones
3-inch T pins
1-inch dressmaker's straight pins

Florist wire
White glue
Drill
Acrylic paint and a small brush
Clear plastic fishing line

Choose a pinecone or buckeye to form an appropriate size body. Attach arms and legs by either pushing a T pin through soft hemlock cones or nuts and pinning this row of nuts to the body, or by stringing florist wire through holes already drilled in acorns. The T in the T pins will keep the hemlock cones on, or you may bend the end of the florist wire so that the nuts do not drop off. The figure's head, consisting of a walnut, acorn, buckeye, or other nut, is attached by sticking a T pin through it and pinning it to the body. Glue may be used to help hold the head in place. Ears or nose may be added by pinning hemlock cones or small acorns to the head. (The drill is only necessary when the nut is too hard to push a pin through.) The face may be painted with acrylic paint, and halves of walnuts or pieces of pinecones can be glued on for hats. Nut people can be hung from clear plastic fishing line or florist wire.

Contributed by Mr. Douglas Canady
Williamsburg, Virginia

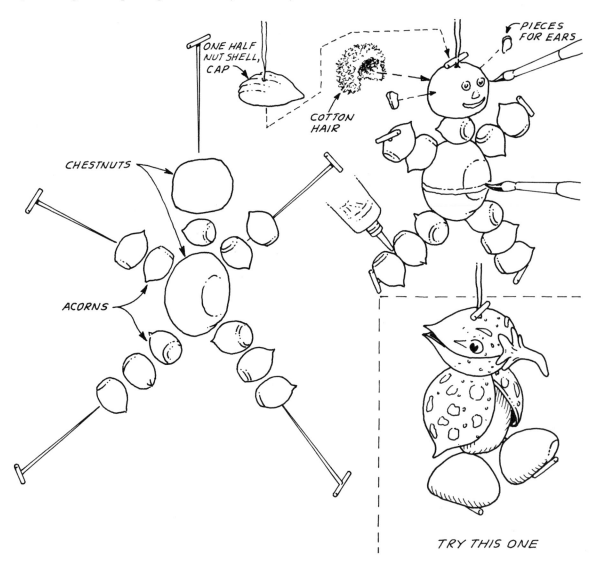

TRY THIS ONE

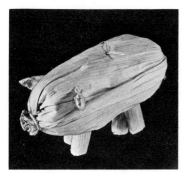

JERRY'S CORNSHUCK PIG

3-inch long ear of corn, such as a
    small ear of popcorn, with the
    husks still attached
Knife

Water
Straight pin
White glue
Thread

Carefully remove the corncob, but leave the husks attached to the base. Trim off all but 2½ inches from the pointed end of the corncob and remove the kernels of corn. Dampen the husks. Slip the cob inside the husks, pointed end first. Pull the ends of the husks together and twist or braid them. Curl to form a tail. Secure with a pin until dry enough to glue together.

Trim the base end of the cornshuck to form a snout. Cut a cornstalk in 4 equal lengths for legs. Be sure they are in proportion to the body. Glue them to the dry body. Cut a shorter cornstalk and split it to make 2 ears. Glue in place.

NOTE: You may need to tie a bit of thread around the nose if the husks come loose from the base.

Contributed by Mr. Jerry Carr
Smithfield, Virginia

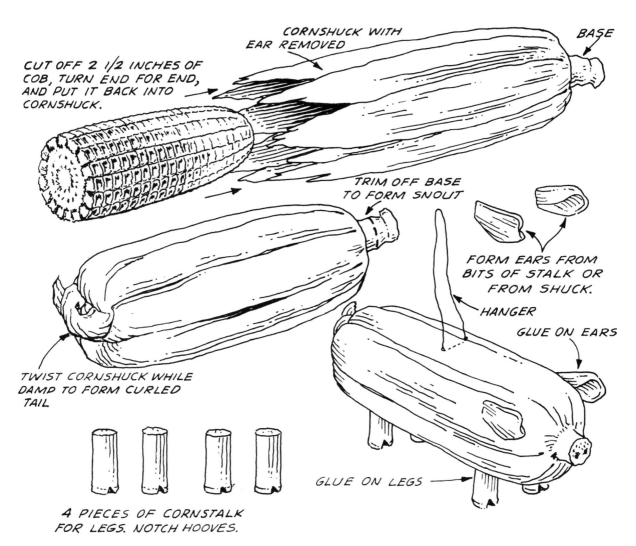

CORNSHUCK WITH EAR REMOVED

BASE

CUT OFF 2 1/2 INCHES OF COB, TURN END FOR END, AND PUT IT BACK INTO CORNSHUCK.

TRIM OFF BASE TO FORM SNOUT

FORM EARS FROM BITS OF STALK OR FROM SHUCK.

HANGER

GLUE ON EARS

TWIST CORNSHUCK WHILE DAMP TO FORM CURLED TAIL

GLUE ON LEGS

4 PIECES OF CORNSTALK FOR LEGS. NOTCH HOOVES.

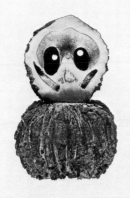

BLACK WALNUT OWL

2 medium-size black walnut shells,
    thoroughly dried
Small wire brush
Pliers or bench vise
Small hand or electric saw
Straight pin

Medium grade sandpaper or file
Household cement
Tiny eye screw
Metal or yarn hanger
Optional—hand or electric drill

Select medium-size black walnut shells. You will need ½ shell for the head and a whole walnut for the body. Note that regular walnuts cannot be used. Clean the shells with a wire brush. Cut 1 shell into 2 equal parts following the seam line as closely as possible. To cut, place the shell in a bench vise and saw with either a hand saw or an electric saw. Or hold the shell with pliers and feed it into the saw blade very slowly. (Don't try to hold the shell in your hand; you may cut your finger.)

Clean out the meat from the split walnut with a straight pin. Sand the cut side of this shell to eliminate saw marks. Sand the top of the whole shell and the bottom of the half shell to obtain the smooth surface needed for gluing together. The bottom of the body can also be sanded smooth to allow the owl to stand alone. Using a vise to hold the head, drill a small hole for an eye screw at the top of head. Glue the head to the body with household cement and let it set for about 10 hours. Add a metal or yarn hanger.

You can drill small holes in the back of the head through the eye holes to allow light to shine through.

Contributed by Mr. P.A.T. Bibb
Roanoke, Virginia

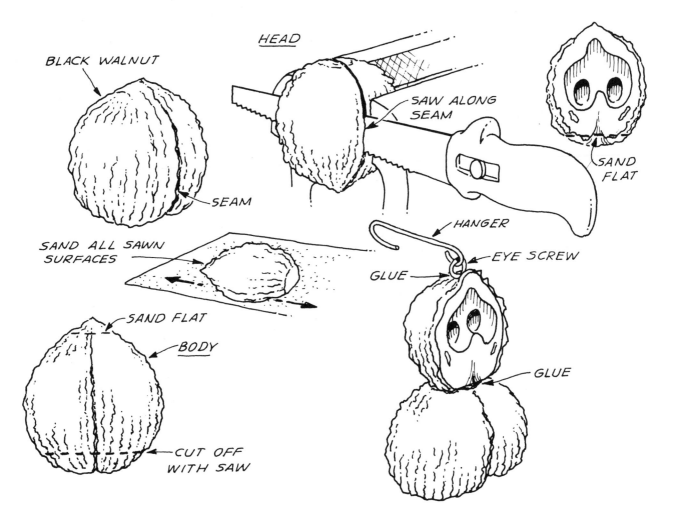

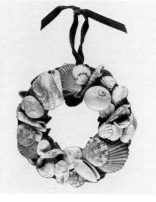

SHELL WREATH

X-acto knife or sturdy scissors
Corrugated cardboard (4 inches x 4 inches x ¼ inch thick–2 thin pieces can be glued together)

Household cement
Red velvet ribbon, ¼ inch wide and 24 inches long
Shells in assorted sizes

With the X-acto knife or the scissors, cut the cardboard into a circle 4 inches in diameter, then cut a circle 2 inches in diameter out of the center. Glue a piece of the velvet ribbon around the outside edge of the circle. Glue the rest of the ribbon through the center and tie it into a bow for a hanger.

Using shells picked up at the beach, or purchased, start at the top of the circle and glue on 1 of the larger shells. Glue other larger shells around the edges at well-spaced intervals. Then put in shells of all kinds, textures, sizes, and colors to form a pleasing pattern. Use pieces of spiral coral and tiny shells to fill in any gaps. No 2 wreaths will be alike.

Contributed by Mrs. Neal Wood
St. Louis, Missouri

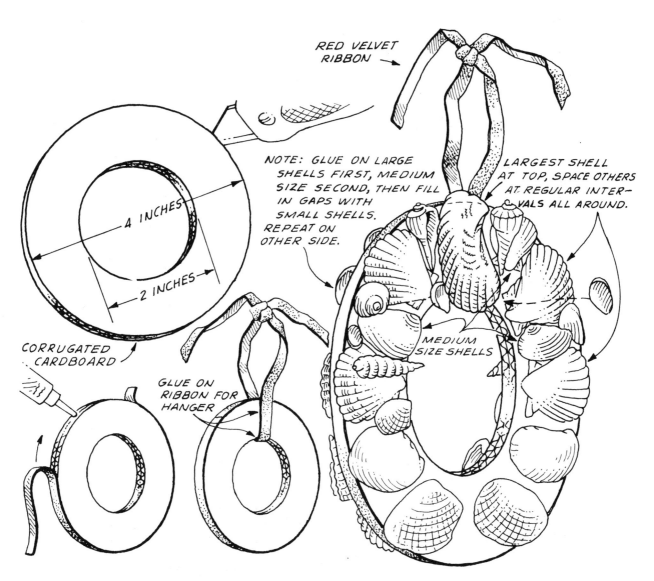

RED VELVET RIBBON →

NOTE: GLUE ON LARGE SHELLS FIRST, MEDIUM SIZE SECOND, THEN FILL IN GAPS WITH SMALL SHELLS. REPEAT ON OTHER SIDE.

LARGEST SHELL AT TOP, SPACE OTHERS AT REGULAR INTERVALS ALL AROUND.

4 INCHES

2 INCHES

MEDIUM SIZE SHELLS

CORRUGATED CARDBOARD

GLUE ON RIBBON FOR HANGER

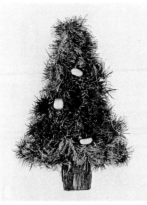

BURR CHRISTMAS TREE

45 burrs
Thin cardboard
Ruler
Pencil
Scissors
Hole punch
Paper clip

Transparent tape
White glue
Thin strips of bark (a 2 inch x 2 inch
 piece of cedar bark makes 1 tree)
Dried corn kernels or red berries
White thread

Pick the burrs early in the fall so that they are still fresh and not brittle. They will not mat together if they are kept on their branches and are picked off 1 at a time as needed.

Cut thin cardboard to form a triangle 5 inches x 4 inches with a base 1 inch x 1 inch. Punch a hole 1 inch down from the top of the triangle. Open the paper clip, insert 1 end into the hole, and tape down to make a hanger. Glue the bark to the base, trimming as needed.

Starting at the widest part of the triangle, glue the burrs to the cardboard in a line. Use a scrap piece of

cardboard to press them down firmly so they won't stick to your hands. Let dry; fill in any holes with individual burrs. Glue on corn kernels or red berries for decoration. Repeat on the other side.

String a piece of thread through the paper clip for a hanger. Store the finished trees in individual plastic bags.

Contributed by Owagena 4-H Club
Cazenovia, New York

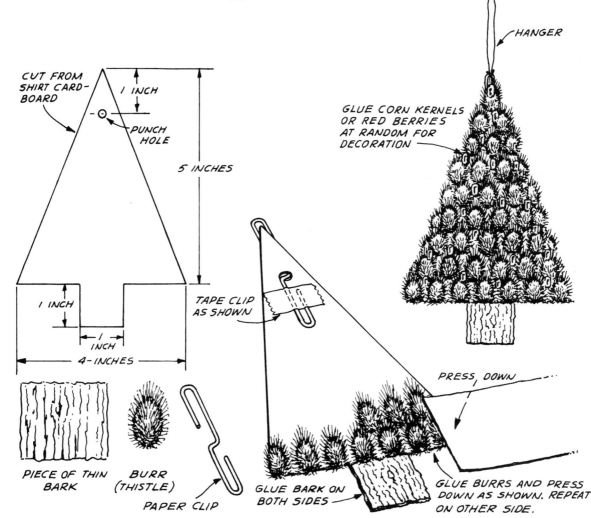

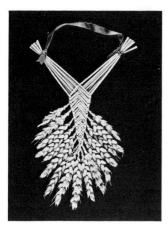

WELSH BORDER FAN

17 evenly matched wheat straws with
 good ears
Straw colored thread
Scissors
Red satin ribbon, ¼ inch wide and
 ½ yard long

Grade the straws according to the size of the ear; begin working with the largest. Tie 3 straws together just below the ears and lay them flat on a table. Spread out the 3, then follow the drawings below.

Insert a straw under A and over B, then another under C and over the one just inserted. Push together. These new straws are locked into position by taking the outside straw (A) and bending it back and under the second straw (B), allowing it to lie to the left. Do the same locking movement with straw C, allowing it to lie to the right. Push together. Repeat this locking movement on both sides with the outside straws, making sure that, having passed under the second straw, the outside straws lie on top of the other. Insert another straw at the right

and lock it into place immediately. Do the same on the left. Insert a straw and lock immediately. Then lock each side again. This action of inserting new straws and locking twice is repeated until all of the straws have been used. The locking movement is repeated 4 times before the ends are gathered together at each side, tied off, and cut evenly.

A 2-straw braid or a red ribbon can be used for hanging, and bows can be added.

NOTE: Attention needs to be paid to detail in this design. Evenly matched straws, carefully graded and placed ears, close working, and neatly angled corners will enhance the finished effect.

Contributed by Miss Jane Fuell
Wolverhampton, England

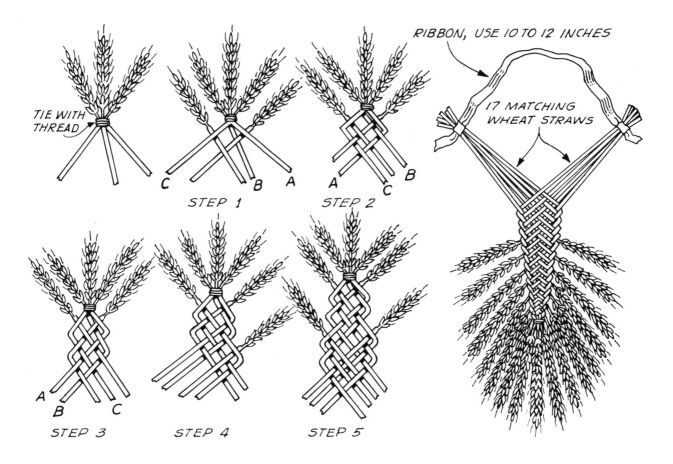

TIE WITH THREAD

C B A STEP 1

A B C STEP 2

RIBBON, USE 10 TO 12 INCHES

17 MATCHING WHEAT STRAWS

A B C STEP 3

STEP 4

STEP 5

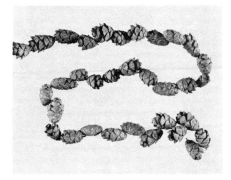

HEMLOCK STRING

Long, sharp needle
Lightweight clear plastic fishing line
Dried hemlock cones

Thread the needle and push it through 1 hemlock cone. Tie the fishing line firmly around the first cone to secure it. Thread the rest of the cones onto the fishing line and secure the last cone as you did the first. String the cones through the middle or end to end. Make the chain as long as you wish.

Contributed by Ms. Ann Brown
Williamsburg, Virginia

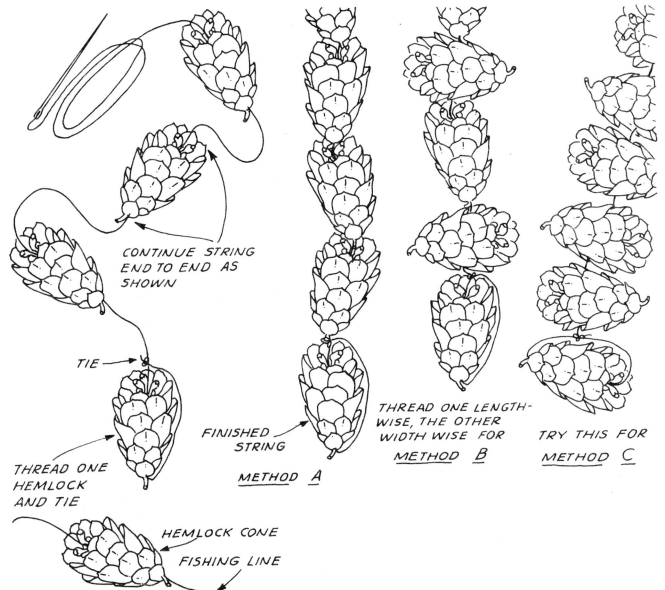

CONTINUE STRING
END TO END AS
SHOWN

TIE

THREAD ONE
HEMLOCK
AND TIE

FINISHED
STRING

METHOD *A*

THREAD ONE LENGTH-
WISE, THE OTHER
WIDTH WISE FOR
METHOD *B*

TRY THIS FOR
METHOD *C*

HEMLOCK CONE

FISHING LINE

START HERE

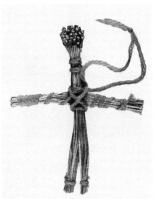

PINE NEEDLE MAN

60 long pine needles
Yarn
Scissors

Collect about 60 dried pine needles. Assemble 30 needles with their woody ends together at the top and tie securely with yarn directly under the woody ends. Tie another piece of yarn ½ inch below the first yarn tie, making sure the knots are to the back.

Assemble the other bunch of needles to form arms. Tie securely by wrapping yarn around them diagonally. Cut off excess needle ends.

Separate in half the section of the body below the yarn. Slip the arms into the separation and tie with yarn by criss crossing the yarn strands to hold the arms securely in place. Knot firmly in back.

Divide the needles below the yarnlike vest and tie the ends to form legs. Trim excess needles and add a yarn hanger.

Contributed by Ms. Cathy Gibbons
Williamsburg, Virginia

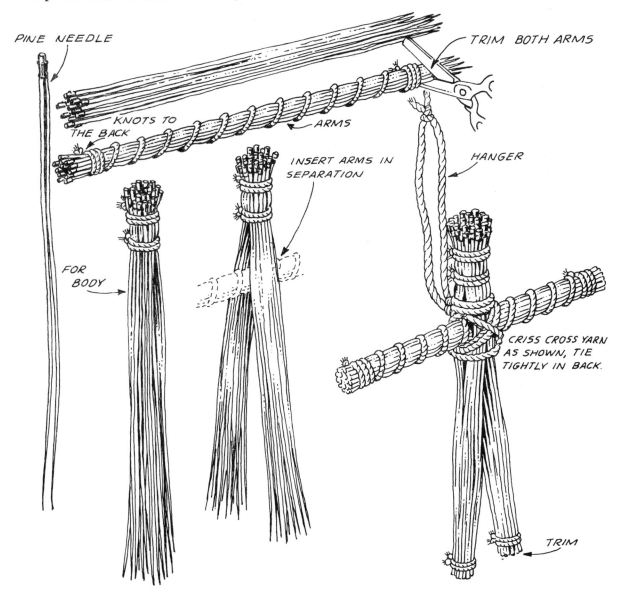

PINE NEEDLE

TRIM BOTH ARMS

KNOTS TO THE BACK

ARMS

INSERT ARMS IN SEPARATION

HANGER

FOR BODY

CRISS CROSS YARN AS SHOWN, TIE TIGHTLY IN BACK.

TRIM

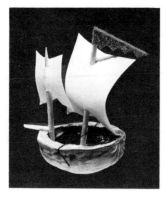

WALNUT BOAT

Walnut
Coping saw
Sandpaper
2 round toothpicks
Household cement

White paper
Scissors
Tiny piece of felt or other fabric
   suitable for a pennant
Black thread

Saw the walnut in half at the seam and remove the meat and fibers. Sandpaper any rough areas. Break off ½ inch from 1 toothpick and glue it to the front of the walnut for a bowsprit. Break off ¼ inch from the other toothpick. This will give you the 2 masts, 1 of which will be ¼ inch shorter than the other. Fill the boat about ¼ full of household cement. Let dry partially.

While the glue is hardening, cut 2 sails, 1 larger than the other, from the white paper. Make 2 tiny holes in each as shown below. Thread the taller toothpick through the larger sail, the shorter through the smaller sail.

Glue a small felt or fabric pennant at the top of the taller mast.

Push the masts into the glue, with the shorter mast in front by the bowsprit and the taller in the center. The sails should curve toward the back of the boat. Add more glue, filling the boat about ⅔ full. Cut an 8-inch piece of black thread and press ½ inch of each end into the glue at each mid-side for a hanger. Let dry. Check the masts to be sure they dry parallel.

VARIATIONS: One mast with a triangular sail will make a sailboat. Or put several small square sails on a full-length toothpick mast for a tall ship.

Contributed by Mrs. Susan H. Rountree
Williamsburg, Virginia

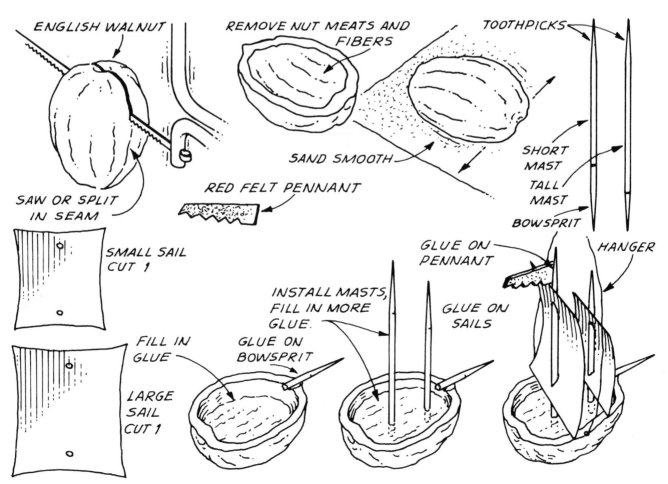

ENGLISH WALNUT

REMOVE NUT MEATS AND FIBERS

TOOTHPICKS

SAW OR SPLIT IN SEAM

SAND SMOOTH

RED FELT PENNANT

SHORT MAST

TALL MAST

BOWSPRIT

SMALL SAIL CUT 1

GLUE ON PENNANT

HANGER

INSTALL MASTS, FILL IN MORE GLUE.

GLUE ON SAILS

FILL IN GLUE

GLUE ON BOWSPRIT

LARGE SAIL CUT 1

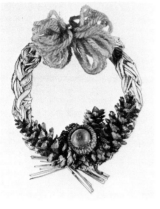

WREATH OF BRAIDED HAY

Supply of hay (dried grasses, stalks of clover, etc., used for fodder)
Newspaper
Fine pliable wire

Assortment of small pinecones, acorns, nuts, seed pods, dried flowers, etc.
White glue
Ribbon or colored yarn for bow

Soak the hay in water overnight to make it pliable. Discard any very thick or very stiff stalks. Lay it in straight strands on the newspaper and work with it while it is quite damp.

Gather a bunch of stalks of uneven lengths (about 1½ inches in diameter) and tie tightly about 1 inch from the top with a few twists of wire, leaving an end of wire about 6–8 inches long. Divide the stalks into 3 sections and braid tightly. Keep the braid flat and shape it into a curve as you go. When 2 inches are left in a section, add another bunch of damp hay about the same thickness, overlap the first strands, and continue braiding it in. Try not to add additional lengths all in the same place, but stagger them so that the slight extra thickness will be distributed evenly.

When the circle is the size desired (approximately 6 inches in diameter), cross the ends over the beginning ends and wire them together tightly with the remaining 6–8 inches of wire. Let the wreath air dry for a day.

Arrange the pods, cones, and other materials into little clumps or sprays and wire them onto the dry wreath at the top, along one side, or wherever they look best. Use glue to help hold the natural materials in place. Finish off the wreath by using a bow of ribbon or several strands of bright yarn to cover where the wire joins. Add wire for a hanger.

Contributed by Mrs. Marie Samford
Williamsburg, Virginia

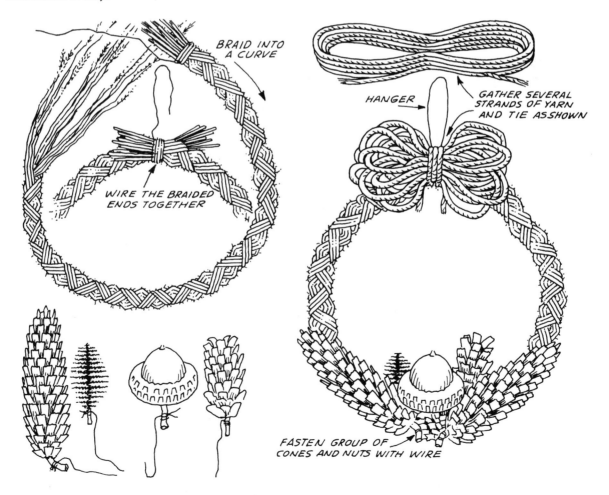

BRAID INTO A CURVE

WIRE THE BRAIDED ENDS TOGETHER

HANGER

GATHER SEVERAL STRANDS OF YARN AND TIE AS SHOWN

FASTEN GROUP OF CONES AND NUTS WITH WIRE

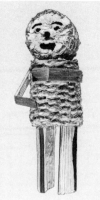

CORNCOB PIG AND MAN

Thick corncob
Jackknife
Black paint and brush or fine felt
    tipped marking pen
Cornstalk or small wooden sticks (for
    legs)

Household cement
Wild grapevine tendril (for tail)
Small eye screw
Lightweight clear plastic fishing line

Pig—Cut a 3-inch-long section of a dried corncob and square off one end so that it is flat. Whittle the other end to form a snout. Paint eyes and nose on the snout with black paint or use the marking pen. Cut 4 1-inch sections of cornstalk or sticks to form legs and glue to the body with household cement. Cut two small triangles of cornstalk and glue onto the head for ears. Glue a small curly section of grapevine tendril to the back end of the pig for a tail. Screw a tiny eye screw into the middle of the back and attach a piece of fishing line for a hanger.

Man—Cut a 1½-inch section of a corncob for the

body. For the head, cut a 1-inch section of corncob, turn it on its side, and glue it to the 1½-inch section. Paint on a face. Glue 2 2-inch cornstalks to the bottom of the corncob to form legs. Split a 1-inch piece of cornstalk in quarters and glue 2 pieces to the side of the body to form arms. The cornstalks can be bent slightly at the ends to look like hands. Screw a tiny screw into the top of the head and attach a piece of fishing line for a hanger.

Contributed by Mr. Osborne Taylor
Toano, Virginia

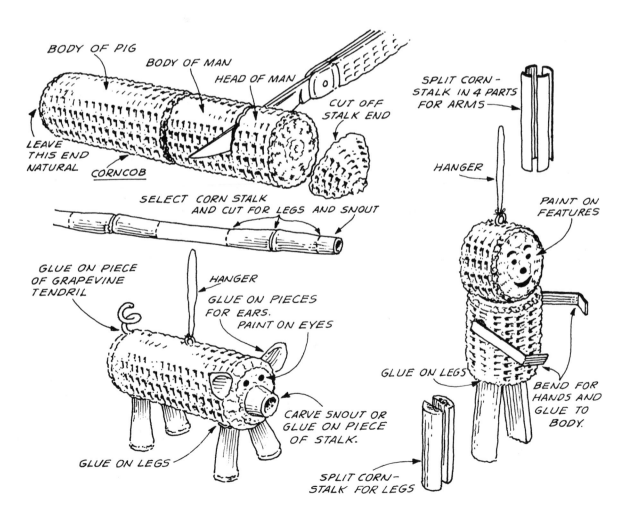

BODY OF PIG

BODY OF MAN

HEAD OF MAN

CUT OFF STALK END

LEAVE THIS END NATURAL

CORNCOB

SPLIT CORN-STALK IN 4 PARTS FOR ARMS

HANGER

SELECT CORN STALK AND CUT FOR LEGS AND SNOUT

PAINT ON FEATURES

GLUE ON PIECE OF GRAPEVINE TENDRIL

HANGER

GLUE ON PIECES FOR EARS. PAINT ON EYES

GLUE ON LEGS

BEND FOR HANDS AND GLUE TO BODY.

GLUE ON LEGS

CARVE SNOUT OR GLUE ON PIECE OF STALK.

SPLIT CORN-STALK FOR LEGS

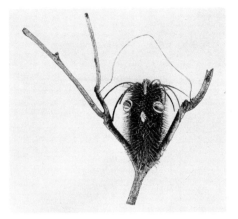

TEASEL OWL

Dried teasel
Scissors or clippers
3 dried sunflower seeds
White glue

Small Y-shaped branch
Red ribbon, ¼ inch wide by 12 inches
   long
Red thread

Dry the teasel, then snip the stem as closely to the teasel as possible. Turn it upside down so that the owl will look as if it has hair. Being careful not to prick yourself or break the teasel, glue 2 eyes and a nose onto the teasel using the sunflower seeds. Insert the nose into the teasel horizontally so that one end projects. Hold the seeds in place a few minutes until they begin to dry.

Glue the owl in the crotch of the Y-shaped branch, holding it in position until dry. Tie the ribbon around the vertical stem of the branch below the tree and attach the thread to both diagonal branches for hanging.

Contributed by Senior Girl Scout Troop #339
Cazenovia, New York

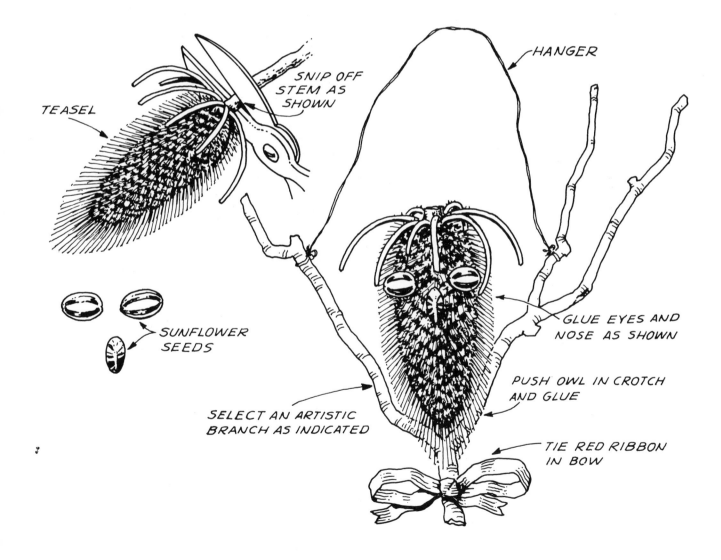

TEASEL

SNIP OFF STEM AS SHOWN

SUNFLOWER SEEDS

SELECT AN ARTISTIC BRANCH AS INDICATED

HANGER

GLUE EYES AND NOSE AS SHOWN

PUSH OWL IN CROTCH AND GLUE

TIE RED RIBBON IN BOW

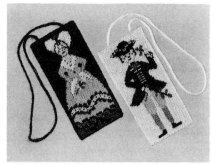

NEEDLEPOINT GEORGE AND MARTHA

MATERIALS: Mono needlepoint canvas, 18 mesh to the inch; masking tape; Paternayan persian yarn, 3-ply, 30-inch strands: 1 #445 dark gold, 4 #453 gold, 1 #455 tan, 7 #012 off-white, 1 #334 dark blue, 3 #330 medium blue, 1 #743 light blue, 6 #R69 red, 1 #287 flesh, 1 #553 green, 1 #144 brown, 2 #050 black; tapestry needle; scissors; matching felt and sewing thread and needle for backing.

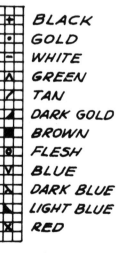

COLOR KEY

- + BLACK
- • GOLD
- − WHITE
- ∧ GREEN
- ∕ TAN
- ◣ DARK GOLD
- ■ BROWN
- ⊙ FLESH
- V BLUE
- ◹ DARK BLUE
- ◥ LIGHT BLUE
- X RED

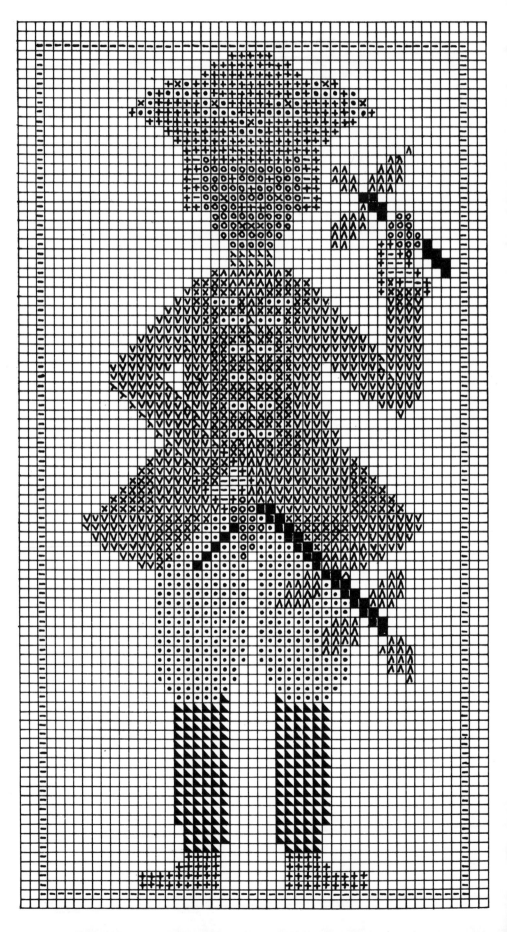

DIRECTIONS: Cut a 4½-inch × 7-inch section of canvas and tape the raw edges with masking tape. Mark the upper right corner of the canvas 1 inch down and 1 inch in from the corner. Using 1 ply of 3-ply yarn, work the design in continental or basketweave (preferable) stitch, following the chart and color key. Fill in the background, which is not completely shown on the chart.

FINISHING: Block. When dry, trim the canvas to within ½ inch of the worked area. Press the raw edges under from the wrong side using a steam iron on wool setting. Overcast the edges with 2 plies of the background yarn. With sewing thread, slip stitch felt backing to the wrong side of the needlepoint. Insert the ends of 1 full 3-ply strand into the top corners for a hanger. The finished size will be 2½ inches × 5 inches.

These decorative panels were inspired by a colorful Pennsylvania fraktur drawing in the Folk Art Collection.

Contributed by The Workbasket
Spring Lake, New Jersey

COLOR KEY

+ BLACK
• GOLD
- WHITE
∧ GREEN
⁄ TAN
⌐ DARK GOLD
■ BROWN
◉ FLESH
∨ BLUE
⊠ DARK BLUE
⊿ LIGHT BLUE
⊠ RED

MINI-CHRISTMAS TREE STOCKING

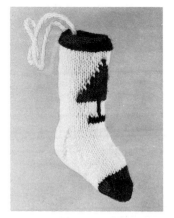

Hunter green and white baby or sock
  yarn, or other fine yarn
1 pair of #1 knitting needles
Tape measure
Tapestry needle

Cuff—Cast on 37 Sts. using hunter green. K. in garter St. (K. every row) for 6 rows. Change to white. P. 1 row, K. 1 row, P. 1 row. Start the tree design. K. 18 Sts. in white. Start design (see diagram below) on next St. and follow the chart for 22 rows in stockinette St. (K. 1 row, P. 1 row). Continue in stockinette St. until the piece measures 2½ inches from the top. Decrease 1 St. on last K. row. 36 Sts. remain. End with a P. row.

Heel—Row 1. K. 10, turn. Row 2. Slip 1, P. 9. Repeat these 2 rows 6 more times (14 rows), ending on a P. row. To turn heel, K. 2, slip 1, K. 1, PSSO, K. 1, turn. Slip 1, P. 3, K. 3, slip 1, K. 1, PSSO, K. 1, turn. Slip 1, P. 4. K. 4, slip 1, K. 1, PSSO, K. 1, turn. Slip 1, P. 5. K. 5, slip 1, K. 1, PSSO (6 Sts. left on needle). Pick up and K. 8 Sts. along the side of this heel piece. Place a marker on the needle, then K. across 16 Sts. of the instep. Place marker. K. remaining 10 Sts. K. in stockinette St. on these 10 Sts. for 14 rows, ending with a K. row. Slip the first stitch of every K. row. *To turn heel,* P. 2, P. 2 tog., P. 1, turn. Slip 1, K. 3. P. 3, P. 2 tog., P. 1, turn. Slip 1, K. 4. P. 4, P. 2 tog., P. 1, turn. Slip 1, K. 5. P. 5, P. 2 tog. (6 Sts. left on needle). Pick up and P. 8

Sts. along the side of this heel piece. P. across the remaining Sts.

Shape heel gusset—K. to within 3 Sts. of the first marker. K. 2 tog. K. 1, slip marker, K. 16, slip marker, K. 1, slip 1, K. 1, PSSO, K. across row. P. 1 row. Repeat these 2 rows until 36 Sts. remain on the needle. Remove the markers. Continue in stockinette St. for 2½ inches, measuring from the back of the heel. End with a K. row.

Shape toe—P. 9 Sts. Place a marker. P. 18 Sts. Place a marker. P. across the remaining 9 Sts. Change to green. K. to within 3 Sts. of the first marker. K. 2 tog., K. 1, slip marker. K. 1, slip 1, K. 1, PSSO, K. to within 3 Sts. of the second marker. K. 2 tog. K. 1, slip marker. K. 1, slip 1, K. 1, PSSO, K. to the end of the row. P. the next row. Repeat these 2 rows until 12 Sts. remain, ending with a K. row. P. 2 tog. across row (6 Sts. remain). Cut the yarn and draw it through. Sew the back and sole seams together. Tie off or sew in all loose ends.

Draw an 8–10-inch piece of yarn through the top of the sock to use as a hanger.

Contributed by Mrs. Sally Piser
Bay Head, New Jersey

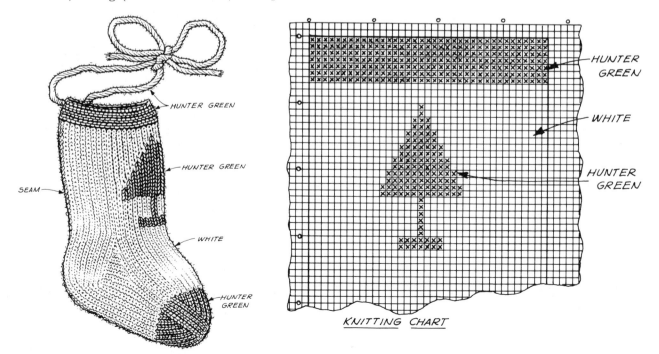

KNITTING CHART

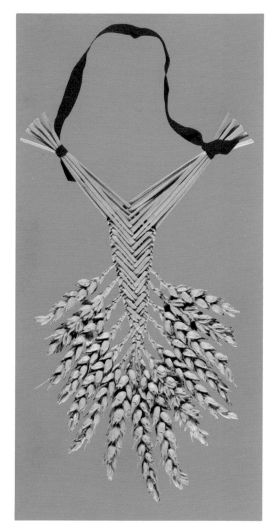

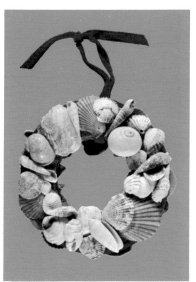

SHELL WREATH, *page 37*

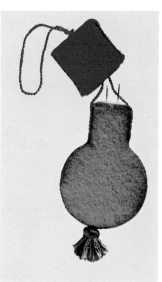

KOREAN NEEDLE CASE, *page 17*

WELSH BORDER FAN, *page 39*

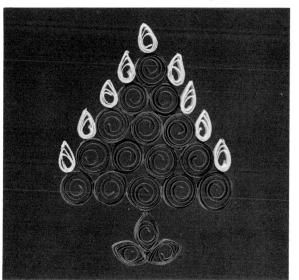

ROLLED PAPER TREE, *page 58*

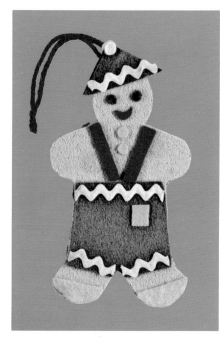

SANDPAPER MAN, *page 56*

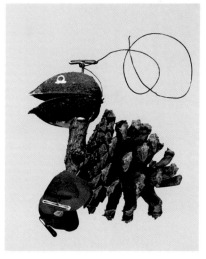

NUT PEOPLE, *page 34*

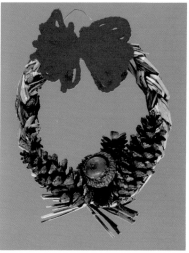

WREATH OF BRAIDED HAY,
page 43

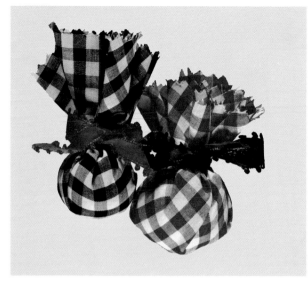

GINGHAM BAG WITH CLOVES, *page 75*

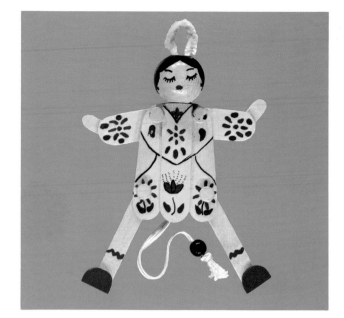

JUMPING JACK DOLL, *page 64*

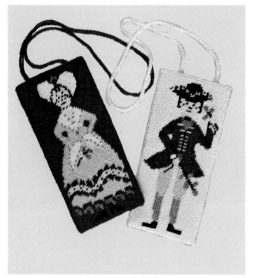

**NEEDLEPOINT GEORGE
AND MARTHA,** *page 46*

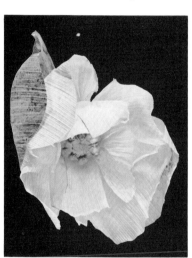

CORNHUSK FLOWER,
page 29

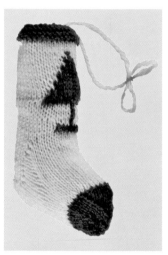

**MINI-CHRISTMAS TREE
STOCKING,** *page 48*

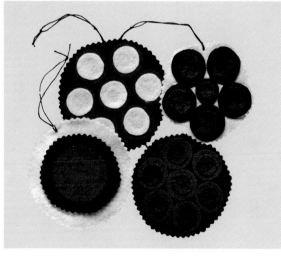

PENNY RUG DESIGNS, *page 21*

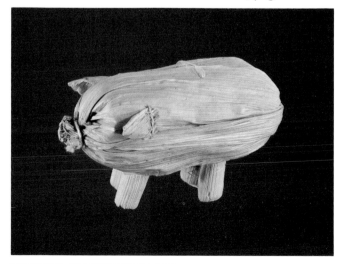

JERRY'S CORNSHUCK PIG, *page 35*

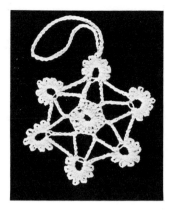

CROCHETED SNOWFLAKE

Size 11 crochet hook
#20 mercerized cotton crochet
    thread
Cork board or heavy cardboard

White paper
Starch
Straight pins (rust proof)

Ch. 10, sl. st. in 1st ch. to form a ring.

Rnd. 1—Ch. 3, make 17 dc. in ring, sl. st. to top of ch. 3.

Rnd. 2—Ch. 1, 1 sc. in 1st dc., 1 sl. st. in same place as sc.* Ch. 12, 1 sc. in 7th ch. from hook. (This makes a picot.) Ch. 5, *skip* 2 dc., 1 sc. in *next* dc. Repeat from * all around, and end the last repeat with sl. st. in first sc. (6 picots)

Rnd. 3—Sl. st. along the ch. 5 *. In the first picot space, work (2 sc., 3 ch.) 7 times, and 2 more sc., ch. 6, repeat from * all around, and end with sl. st. in first sc. Fasten off.

To make a hanger, attach the thread to the top of the fourth picot of any group and make a chain of the length desired. Sl. st. to first ch. and fasten off.

Cover a piece of cork board or heavy cardboard with clean white paper. Dip the snowflake in strong starch, spread to shape on the paper, and pin out all the points evenly. Allow it to dry thoroughly before removing the pins.

NOTE: A larger crochet hook will give a larger snowflake with a lacier look.

HISTORY: *Godey's Lady's Magazine* for December 1866 featured a pattern for a similar crochet design.

Contributed by Mrs. Vi Simms
Williamsburg, Virginia

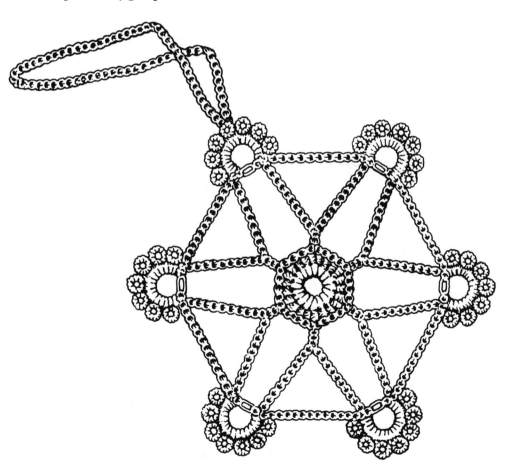

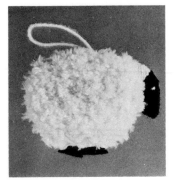

NEEDLEPOINT SHEEP

10 to 12 mesh to the inch needlepoint
  canvas (a piece 6 inches x 8 inches
  makes 1 sheep)
Scissors
Masking tape
Black indelible marking pen
Tapestry yarn: 3 yards black (1
  10-yard skein)

45 yards white (5 10-yard skeins)
Tapestry needle
Black felt scraps (for feet)
Fiberfill, cotton batting, or shredded
  nylon stockings

Cut a 6-inch x 8-inch piece of canvas and tape the raw edges with masking tape. With an indelible marking pen, trace both sides of the sheep onto the canvas as shown. Work the face in black and the ear and eye in white using the tent or half-cross stitch.* The fuzzy part of the sheep is produced by the turkey knot.* To work the body, begin in the lower left area of the sheep and work across the row. At the end of the row, cut the thread, leaving a piece about ½ inch long. Snip all loops across the row. Begin the next row 2 rows above at the left edge of the outline. Work the loops 1 space to the left or right of the loop below. Continue in this fashion, working from left to right within the outline.

When both sides are completed, cut around the sheep ¼ inch from the worked area. Using the pattern given, sew 2 triangles of black felt onto the lower inside of the sheep as shown so that the feet extend below the fuzzy body. Fold the sheep at the center back as shown and turn the edges inside. Overcast all edges in black or white, leaving an opening for stuffing. Stuff lightly and finish the overcasting. Add a yarn hanger.

Tent or half-cross stitch—Diagonally cross over 1 mesh of canvas; insert needle, and bring needle out 1 set of horizontal threads down. Always work from left to right in horizontal rows. Turn upside down, and continue to work from left to right.

Turkey knot—Put needle in at A and under 1 vertical thread to the left. Pull the thread through the canvas, leaving about ½ inch on the front side of the canvas and hold this end with your left thumb. Bring the yarn up and pull tight; hold this working strand above the tightened knot. Put the needle into the canvas at B and up 1 vertical thread to the left (same hole as A) and pull tight. Hold the yarn with your thumb as the needle goes down at C and up 1 hole to the left. Pull until the loop is about ½ inch long. Continue across the row, always working from left to right.

Contributed by Ms. Gail Andrews
Williamsburg, Virginia

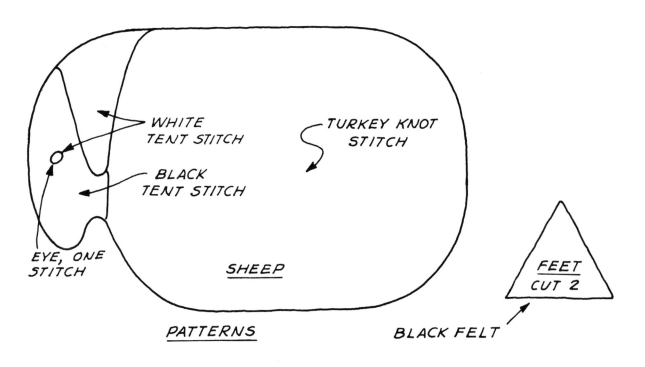

WHITE
TENT STITCH

TURKEY KNOT
STITCH

BLACK
TENT STITCH

EYE, ONE
STITCH

SHEEP

FEET
CUT 2

PATTERNS

BLACK FELT

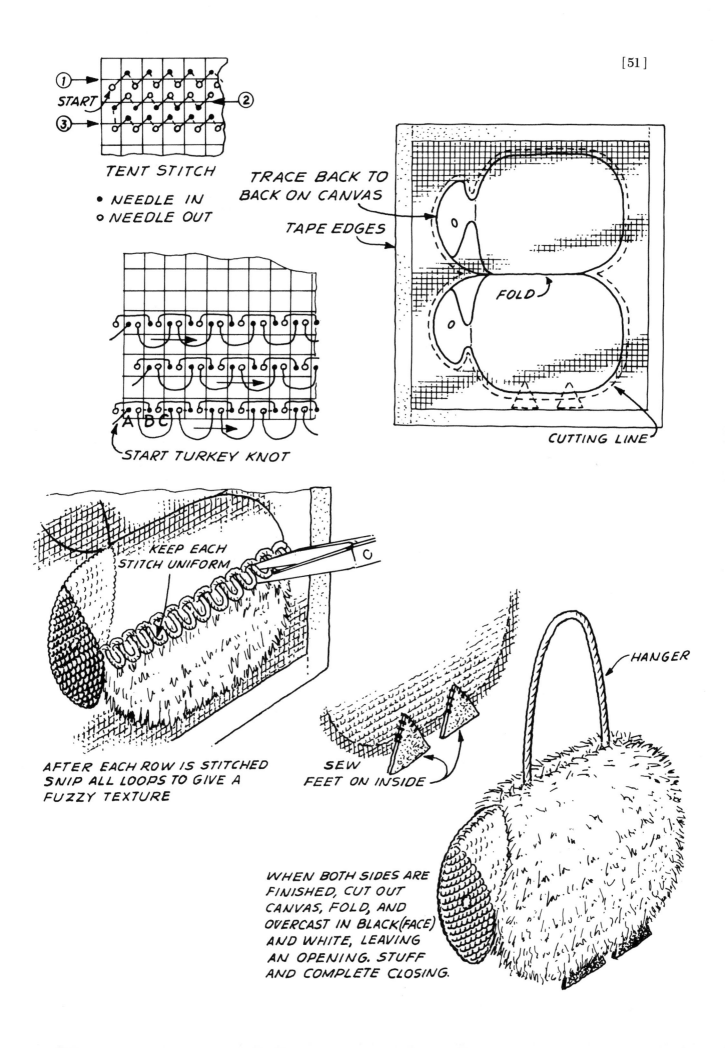

TENT STITCH

• NEEDLE IN
∘ NEEDLE OUT

START TURKEY KNOT

TRACE BACK TO
BACK ON CANVAS

TAPE EDGES

FOLD

CUTTING LINE

KEEP EACH
STITCH UNIFORM

AFTER EACH ROW IS STITCHED
SNIP ALL LOOPS TO GIVE A
FUZZY TEXTURE

SEW
FEET ON INSIDE

HANGER

WHEN BOTH SIDES ARE
FINISHED, CUT OUT
CANVAS, FOLD, AND
OVERCAST IN BLACK(FACE)
AND WHITE, LEAVING
AN OPENING. STUFF
AND COMPLETE CLOSING.

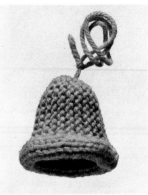

KNITTED YARN BELL

Small Bell:
Baby yarn or other fine yarn
Number 2 needles
Tapestry needle
Metal bell

Large Bell:
4-ply yarn
Number 3 or 4 needles
Tapestry needle
Metal bell

Cast on 14 sts. Row 1: K.10, P 4. Row 2: K.14 (right side). Repeat these 2 rows until you have 22 ridges (44 rows), ending with K.14 row. Bind off, leaving a 12-inch strand of yarn. Sew cast on and bound off edges together. The bottom of the bell has a border of stockinette stitch. To form the top of the bell, thread the tapestry needle with the 12-inch strand of yarn and run it through every other stitch, pulling tightly. Sew the metal bell on the inside. Use the remaining yarn to make a hanging loop.

NOTE: Bells can be decorated with duplicate or other decorative stitches.

Contributed by Mrs. Virginia Roseberg
Williamsburg, Virginia

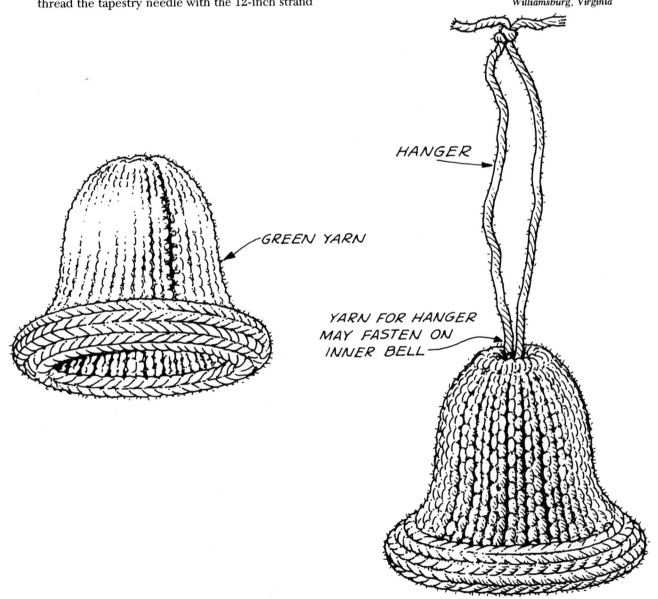

GREEN YARN

HANGER

YARN FOR HANGER
MAY FASTEN ON
INNER BELL

NEEDLEPOINT CORNUCOPIA

12 to 14 mesh to the inch needlepoint
   canvas (a piece 5 inches x 5 inches
   makes 1 cornucopia)
Scissors

Red, green, and white 3-ply persian
   tapestry yarn—8 30-inch strands of
   each color
Tapestry needle
Sewing needle and thread.

Cut a piece of canvas 70 threads square (5 inches x 5 inches). Fold over 4 threads on each side. To reduce thickness at the corners, cut out a small square as shown. Baste the 4 sides in place. Work a row of tent stitch (step 1) using 2 plies of red yarn on the third thread in on all 4 sides. This will keep the edges from fraying. Starting at the upper left corner adjoining the row of tent stitch, work 2 plies of red in the Milanese stitch* diagonally from the upper left to the lower right corner as shown (step 2). Continue to fill in the canvas using the Milanese stitch, turning the canvas upside down (steps 3 and 4) at the end of each row and working back in the next color. Alternate 1 row of red, 1 of green, and 1 of white, then repeat. Be sure the adjoining rows share the same holes (steps 3 and 4). When the design has been completed, overcast sides B and C using a 3-ply strand of green. This will be the opening. Fold sides A and D and whip together in green. Add a loop as shown for a hanger. Fill the cornucopia with candy or small boxes, or leave empty.

Milanese stitch—See diagram. Needle comes up at 1, crosses over and goes down at 2, crosses behind and comes up at 3, goes down at 4, etc.

NOTE: This stitch distorts the canvas, but blocking will help to correct it. The cornucopia can be sewn even if it isn't square.

Contributed by Mrs. Norma Lauer
Williamsburg, Virginia

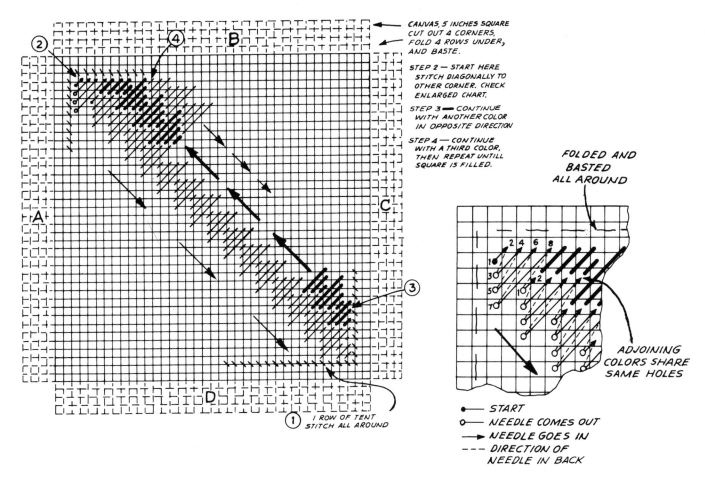

CANVAS, 5 INCHES SQUARE
CUT OUT 4 CORNERS,
FOLD 4 ROWS UNDER,
AND BASTE.

STEP 2 — START HERE
STITCH DIAGONALLY TO
OTHER CORNER. CHECK
ENLARGED CHART.

STEP 3 — CONTINUE
WITH ANOTHER COLOR
IN OPPOSITE DIRECTION

STEP 4 — CONTINUE
WITH A THIRD COLOR,
THEN REPEAT UNTILL
SQUARE IS FILLED.

FOLDED AND
BASTED
ALL AROUND

ADJOINING
COLORS SHARE
SAME HOLES

1 ROW OF TENT
STITCH ALL AROUND

•— START
○— NEEDLE COMES OUT
→ NEEDLE GOES IN
--- DIRECTION OF
    NEEDLE IN BACK

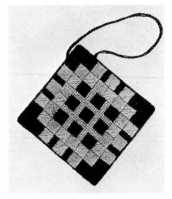

NEEDLEPOINT COVERLET SQUARES

MATERIALS: Interlock needlepoint canvas, 12 mesh to the inch; masking tape; Paternayan persian yarn, 3-ply, 30-inch strands; #321 blue, #240 red, #015 off-white (10 3-ply strands of each of 2 colors complete 1 ornament); tapestry needle; scissors; matching felt and sewing thread and needle for backing.

DIRECTIONS: Cut a 6-inch x 6-inch section of canvas and tape the raw edges with masking tape. Mark the upper right corner of the canvas 1 inch down and 1 inch in from the corner. Using 2 plies of 3-ply yarn, work the design in continental, basketweave, or decorative stitches, following the chart. Use any 2 colors for designs 1, 2, and 3. For No. 4, 3 colors are used.

FINISHING: Block. When dry, trim the canvas to within ½ inch of the worked area. Press the raw edges under from the wrong side using a steam iron on wool setting. Overcast the edges with background yarn, using a full 3-ply strand. With sewing thread, slip stitch felt backing to the wrong side of the needlepoint. The finished size will be 4 inches x 4 inches. Insert the ends of 1 3-ply strand into 1 corner for a hanger.

Contributed by The Workbasket
Spring Lake, New Jersey

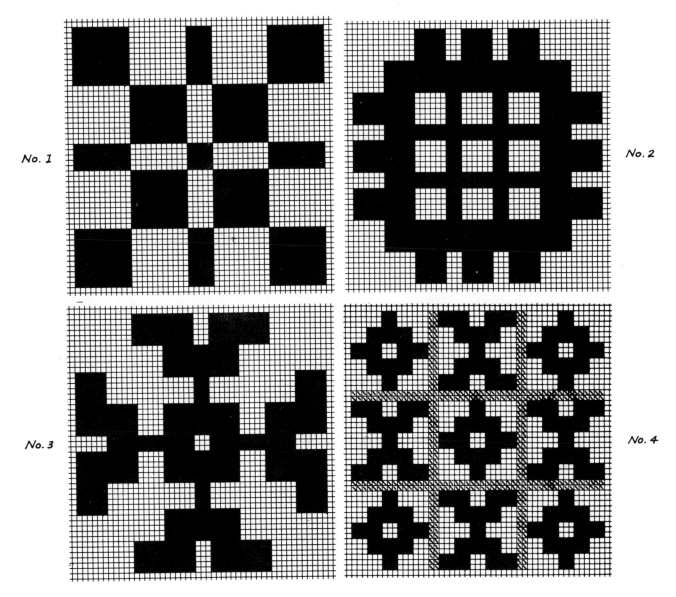

No. 1 No. 2 No. 3 No. 4

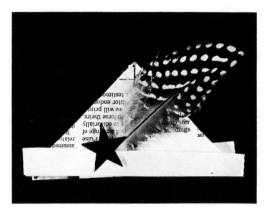

NEWSPAPER SOLDIER HATS

Newspaper
Scissors
Transparent tape

Paper star with sticky back
Small feathers (one for each hat)
Fishing line, string, or thread

Cut out the newspaper to form a rectangle either 3 inches x 2 inches, 5 inches x 4 inches, or 4 inches x 3 inches. Fold it in half widthwise. Take 2 corners of the folded edge and fold forward until they touch in the middle of the paper. Then smooth down the edges. Take the 2 bottom edges and fold upward on the outside to form the brim of the hat. These edges may be taped down with a tiny piece of tape. Tape on a feather below the brim, using a paper star to hold it in place. Suspend the hat from fishing line, string, or thread.

Contributed by Mrs. William Galloway
Hampton, Virginia

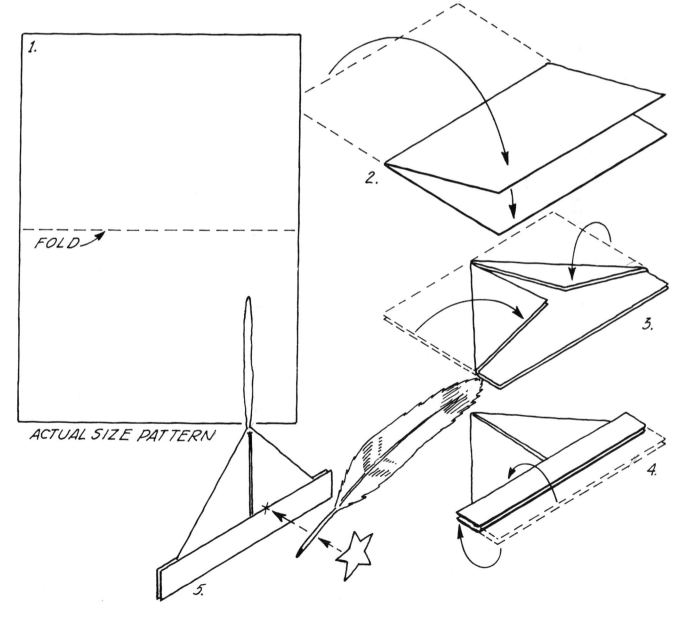

1.

FOLD

ACTUAL SIZE PATTERN

2.

3.

4.

5.

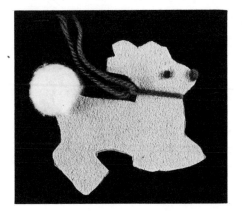

SANDPAPER MAN AND REINDEER

Coarse sandpaper
Pencil
Strong scissors
White glue
Felt scraps—red, green, blue, white,
  and black

Scraps of green medium size
  rick-rack
Yarn
Cotton

Trace the outlines of the gingerbread man and reindeer on the smooth sides of 2 pieces of sandpaper. Cut out both shapes and glue the smooth sides together. Let dry.

Decorate as follows: Use felt for eyes, mouth, hat, trousers, and belt, rick-rack for suspenders, yarn in strips for bangs under the hat, and cotton for a beard. Decorate both sides. Make a yarn loop at the top of the hat for a hanger.

Give the reindeer a cotton tail, a harness made out of rick-rack or yarn, an eye of black felt, and a red felt nose.

These cutouts can be dressed as elaborately as your imagination suggests.

Contributed by Mrs. Charles E. Thwaite III
Atlanta, Georgia

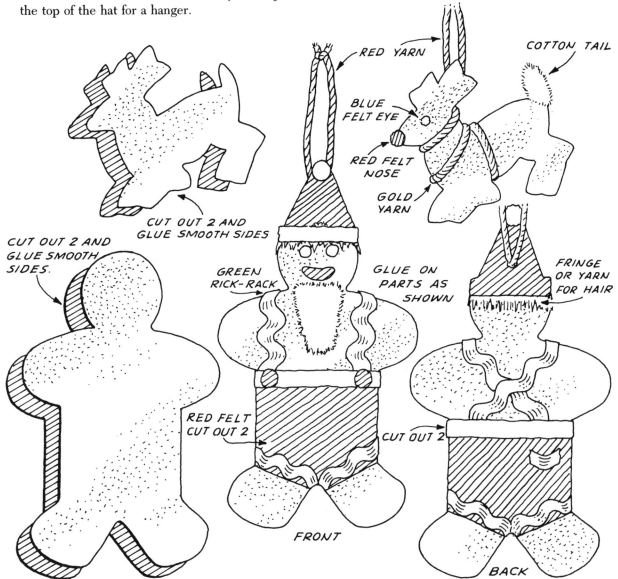

CUT OUT 2 AND GLUE SMOOTH SIDES

RED YARN

COTTON TAIL

BLUE FELT EYE

RED FELT NOSE

GOLD YARN

CUT OUT 2 AND GLUE SMOOTH SIDES.

GREEN RICK-RACK

GLUE ON PARTS AS SHOWN

FRINGE OR YARN FOR HAIR

RED FELT CUT OUT 2

CUT OUT 2

FRONT

BACK

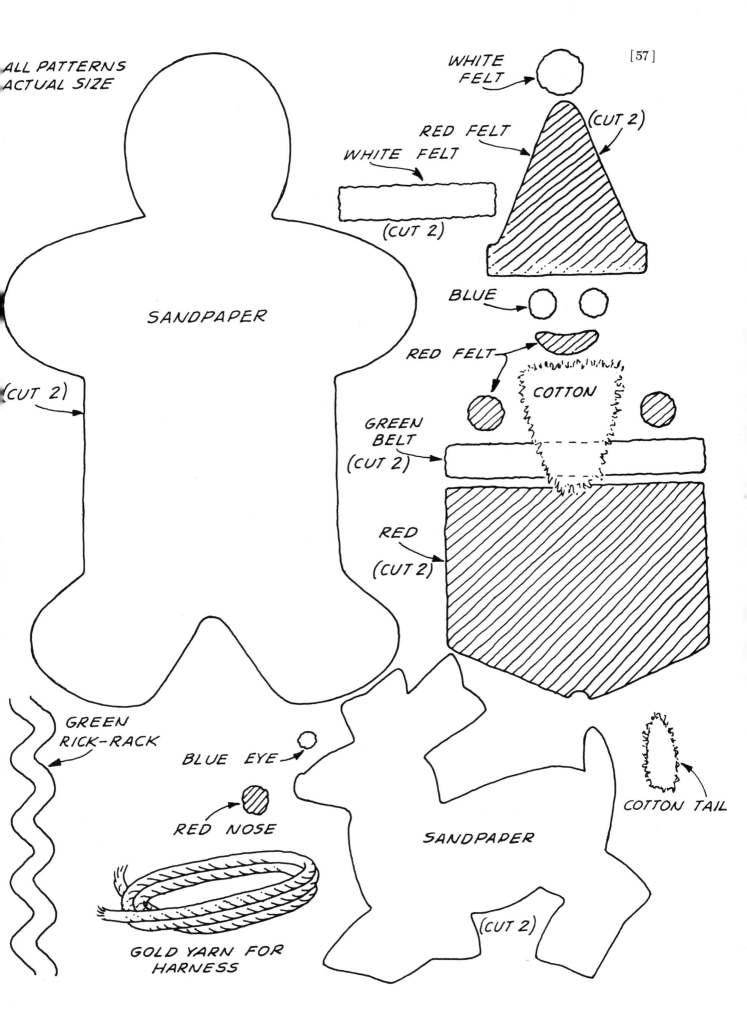

ALL PATTERNS
ACTUAL SIZE

SANDPAPER

(CUT 2)

GREEN
RICK-RACK

BLUE EYE

RED NOSE

GOLD YARN FOR
HARNESS

[57]

WHITE
FELT

RED FELT

WHITE
FELT

(CUT 2)

(CUT 2)

BLUE

RED FELT

COTTON

GREEN
BELT
(CUT 2)

RED

(CUT 2)

COTTON TAIL

SANDPAPER

(CUT 2)

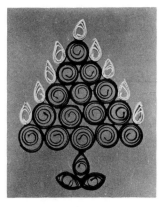

ROLLED PAPER CHRISTMAS TREE

Graph or lined paper
Wax paper
Quilling paper: 18 4-inch pieces of
green
9 2-inch pieces of
yellow

Ruler
Corsage pin or quilling tool
White glue
Toothpick or straight pin
Green thread

Cover a sheet of graph or lined paper with a sheet of wax paper. Measure the required lengths of quilling paper and tear off. Torn ends are less conspicuous. To make a coil, tightly pinch 1 end of 1 strip of paper around the corsage pin or quilling tool. Roll the rest of the strip, but with a looser tension, hold for a moment, then remove from the quilling tool. Allow the coils to unroll until the row is the size desired. Glue the end down, using a toothpick or pin to apply a small amount of glue; hold until the glue sets. Make and glue all coils, being sure that all are uniform in size. Make an eye-shaped piece with 3 of the green coils by gently pinching the opposite sides of the coils while leaving them round in the center. With all of the yellow coils make raindrop shapes by pinching the coils at the end where they are glued. Assemble the 15 round green coils in a pyramid shape and glue together. Glue the 3 eye-shaped pieces together in an inverted T-shape and glue to the tree for the base. Glue the 9 yellow raindrop-shaped coils onto the ends of each row of coils of the tree, adding one on the top. To make a hanger, thread a loop through the top raindrop-shaped coil and knot the ends.

Contributed by Ms. Pat Scott
Oglesby, Illinois

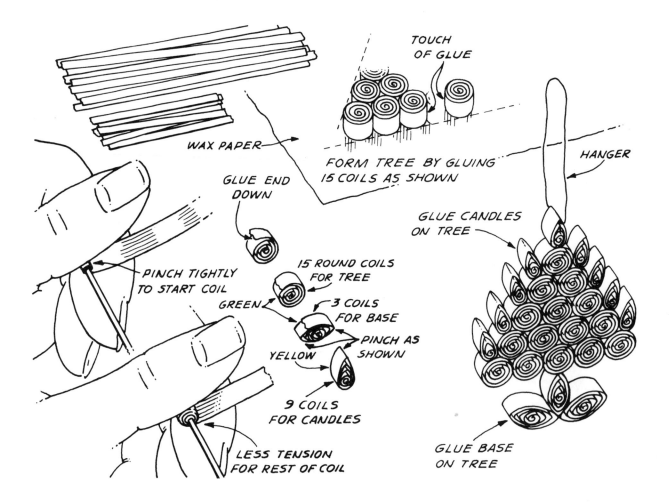

WAX PAPER

TOUCH OF GLUE

FORM TREE BY GLUING 15 COILS AS SHOWN

HANGER

GLUE END DOWN

GLUE CANDLES ON TREE

PINCH TIGHTLY TO START COIL

15 ROUND COILS FOR TREE

GREEN

3 COILS FOR BASE

PINCH AS SHOWN

YELLOW

9 COILS FOR CANDLES

LESS TENSION FOR REST OF COIL

GLUE BASE ON TREE

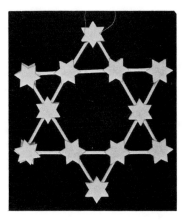

PAPER STARS

6 white paper drinking straws or 3
   long white paper craft straws cut in
   half
White glue
White construction paper
8-inch piece of black thread

Take 3 straws and form a triangle by gluing them
together at the ends. Form another triangle with
the other 3 straws. Let dry. Glue the 2 triangles
together to form a 6-pointed star.

Cut 24 6-pointed small stars from white construction paper and glue them onto both sides of the
straw star where the straws intersect.

Hang with a small loop of black thread.

Contributed by Ms. Gail Andrews
Williamsburg, Virginia

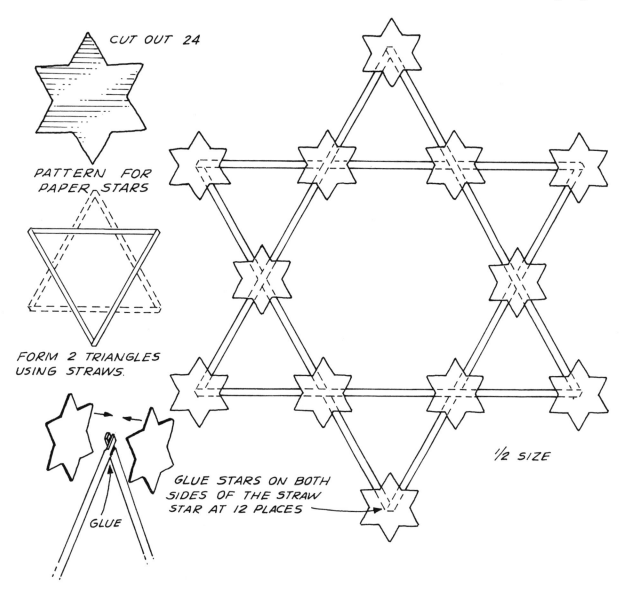

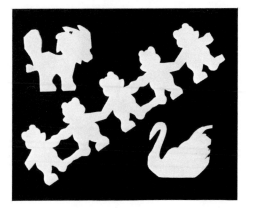

PAPER SILHOUETTES

Colored construction paper
Pencil
Scissors

Decide which figure you want to make. You can make a string of animals, such as bears or elephants, or a set of figures, such as angels or snowmen. Fold the construction paper into several layers wide enough to accommodate the figure you have chosen and thick enough to make the chain the length you desire. On the folded construction paper, trace the pattern given or draw around your favorite cookie cutter.

Cut out the figure, being careful to leave part of the folded area on each side of the shape intact. If the folds are cut through entirely, the figures will not form a chain and will instead be separate and unattached to one another.

After the cutting is completed, open the paper figures and find a chain to surround the tree!

Contributed by Mrs. Judith W. Blood
Far Hills, New Jersey

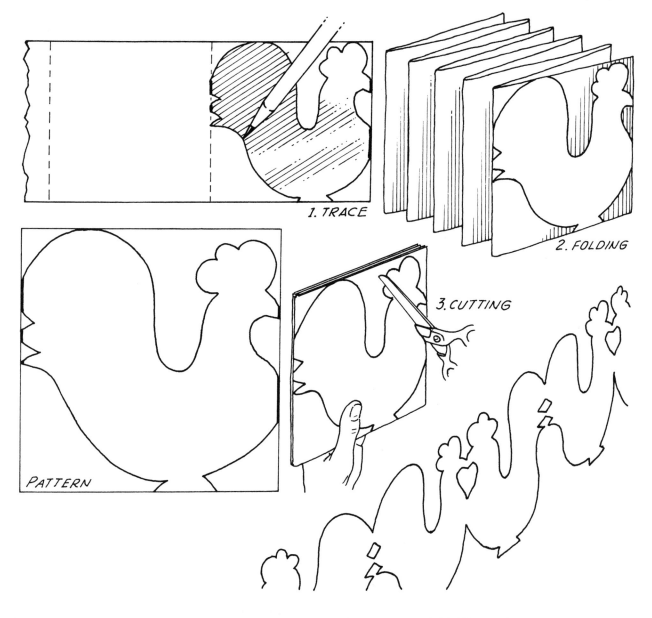

1. TRACE

2. FOLDING

3. CUTTING

PATTERN

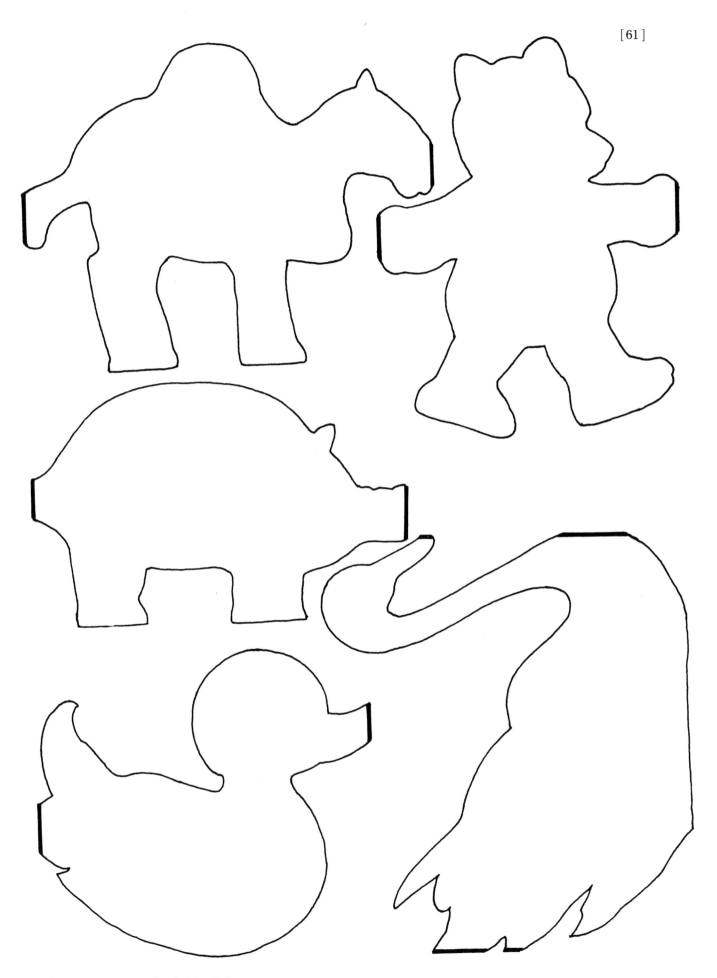

Do not cut on thick black lines.

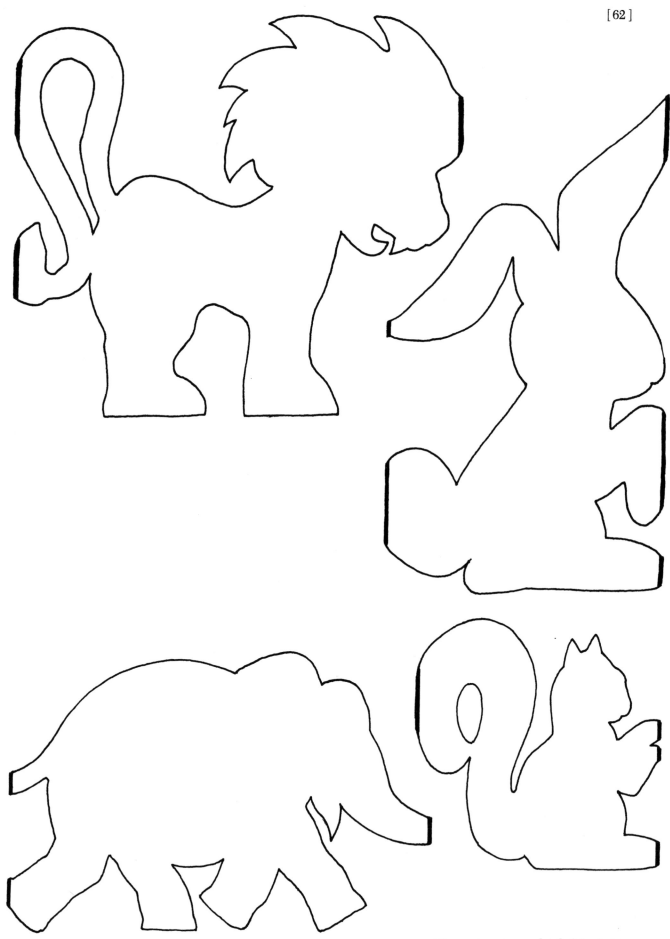

Do not cut on thick black lines.

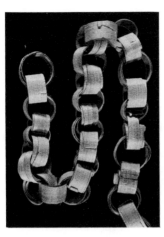

WOOD SHAVINGS CHAIN

Soft piece of wood 11 inches long by
    ¾–1 inch thick
Wood plane (jack plane)
Optional—paper clips

Using a soft piece of wood approximately 11 inches in length and ¾–1 inch thick, plane off thin shavings. When coiled around itself twice, an 11-inch shaving will result in a circle about 1½ inches in diameter. The natural spring of the wood will be enough to hold the shaving in a circle. Stretch out a shaving, and if there is a thicker end, hold it between the thumb and first 2 fingers of your left hand, forming a circle. The next shaving coils through the last one made and so on. No glue is necessary.

NOTE: If you have trouble making a shaving form a circle, you can stretch it out, wrap it around 3 fingers so that it forms a circle 1½ inches in diameter, and clip the inside end to the side with a paper clip. Let it set this way for a day. You may also use a paper clip after the chain is formed to hold a stray end in place until it sets.

Contributed by Mr. Lew LeCompte
Williamsburg, Virginia

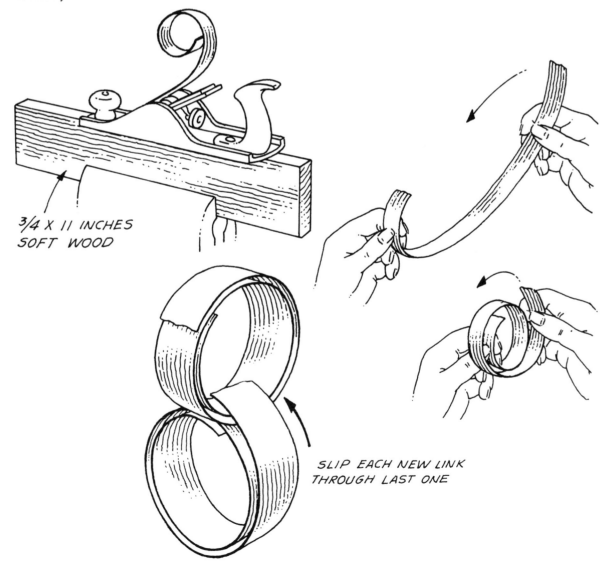

3/4 X 11 INCHES
SOFT WOOD

SLIP EACH NEW LINK
THROUGH LAST ONE

JUMPING JACK DOLL

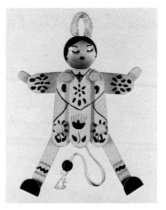

3 wooden tongue depressors (6-inch
   length is best) or 2 tongue
   depressors and 2 popsicle sticks
Pencil
Ruler
Coping saw
Sandpaper or file
Drill with $^1/_{16}$-inch and $^1/_8$-inch bits
Household cement
Paint—yellow, black, red, and green
Very fine brush

Medium brush
1-inch wooden bead for head, natural
   color
4 ½-inch brass paper fasteners
Pipe cleaner
Carpet thread or other heavy thread
   that will tie securely
Tweezers
Metallic string or flat braid (for pull
   string)
Small bead

Draw patterns on the tongue depressors, adjusting them if you can't find large tongue depressors. Measure the parts to make sure that they are the right size. Popsicle sticks cut to the proper length may be used for legs and hands. (This saves the trouble of cutting the tongue depressors in half.)

Cut out the pieces with a coping saw and round the edges where indicated with a file or sandpaper. Smooth all edges with sandpaper.

Very slowly and carefully drill holes for the brass fasteners and the thread connections. Make sure the holes are just a bit larger than the fasteners to allow the fasteners to move easily. Note the off-center positions of the holes.

Glue the hands to the arms, tilted up, noting the left and right hole locations. Glue the shoes to the legs slightly off-center so that the feet extend outward. Glue the center to the sides, the center on top and the sides under, slanting outward at the bottom. Space should be left at the back to insert the ends of the pipe cleaner when the head is glued on later. Let dry.

Paint. Sleeves, dress, and legs—white. Pinafore —2 coats of yellow. Head—black hair and features, red mouth. Heads of brass fasteners—yellow. Hands and face—natural wood color. Dress decorations—red flowers, green leaves. Shoes—red. Legs —red and yellow trim.

Double a pipe cleaner to make a loop at the top of the head. Let the ends extend at least 1 inch below the head and glue them at the back in the space between the 2 side pieces.

Run a thread through the smaller drilled holes in the arms and legs. Insert brass fasteners into the large holes of the legs, arms, and body, and turn down the wings of the fasteners with tweezers. Be sure to leave space for free movement of the arms and legs. Tie the threads with a secure knot while the arms and legs are in a downward position. Tie cording onto the arm thread and leg thread in a single knot. Let the cord extend below the doll's shoes by 3 inches. Thread a small bead onto the cording and knot the end of the cord to hold it.

HISTORY: This animated toy is patterned after one purchased at the annual bazaar sponsored by the women of R. E. Lee Memorial Episcopal Church in Lexington, Virginia. But the Old World prototype for this ever popular plaything dates at least as early as the sixteenth century. German toymakers shipped quantities of the gaily painted, two dimensional, jointed dolls to the United States during the nineteenth century.

Contributed by Mrs. Emily Lancaster
Lexington, Virginia

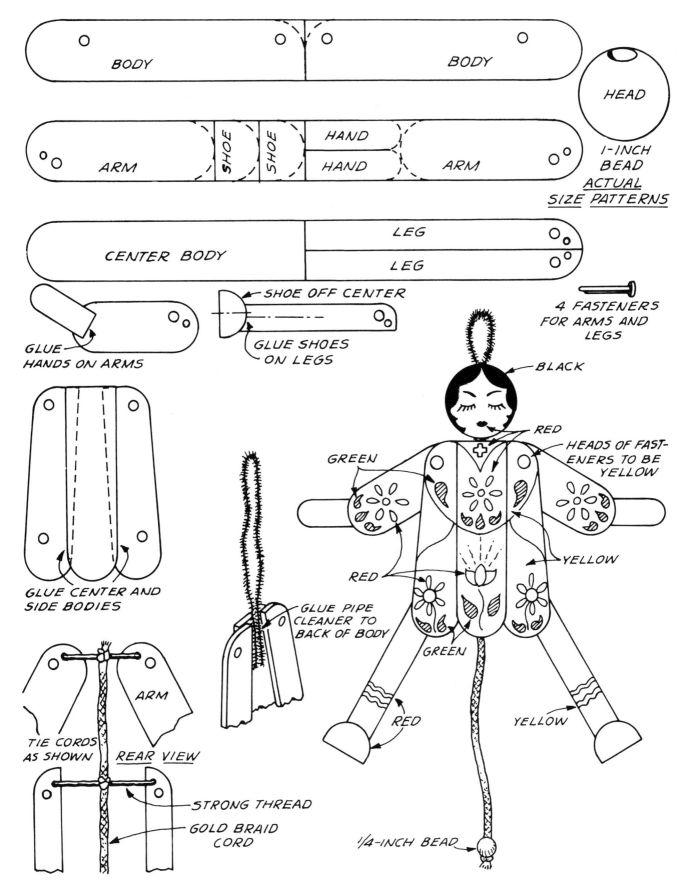

BODY

BODY

HEAD

1-INCH
BEAD
ACTUAL
SIZE PATTERNS

ARM

SHOE

SHOE

HAND

HAND

ARM

LEG

LEG

CENTER BODY

GLUE
HANDS ON ARMS

SHOE OFF CENTER

GLUE SHOES
ON LEGS

4 FASTENERS
FOR ARMS AND
LEGS

BLACK

RED

HEADS OF FAST-
ENERS TO BE
YELLOW

GREEN

YELLOW

RED

GREEN

GLUE CENTER AND
SIDE BODIES

GLUE PIPE
CLEANER TO
BACK OF BODY

RED

YELLOW

TIE CORDS
AS SHOWN

ARM

REAR VIEW

STRONG THREAD

GOLD BRAID
CORD

1/4-INCH BEAD

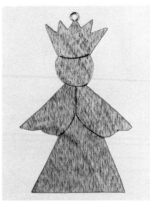

THREE WISE MEN

Pencil
1 piece of white pine, 3 inches x 6
inches x ¼ inch
1 piece of walnut, 3 inches x 6 inches
x ¼ inch (dark stain can be used)
1 piece of red cedar, 3 inches x 6 inches
x ¼ inch (red stain can be used)

Coping saw or electric jig saw
Medium sandpaper or thin file
Electric burning needle
Stain if necessary
Clear finish
Brush
3 eye screws
Lightweight clear plastic fishing line

Trace the figures onto the wood and carefully cut them out with the coping saw or electric jig saw. Different types of wood will produce figures of different colors. Sand the sides and edges of the figures smooth. With an electric burning needle, burn in the features on both sides. Stain if necessary. Attach an eye screw to the top of each figure.

Give the figures 2 coats of clear finish. Insert pieces of fishing line through the eye screws for hangers.

NOTE: Vary the details of their robes with the burning needle.

Contributed by Mr. William Blair
Williamsburg, Virginia

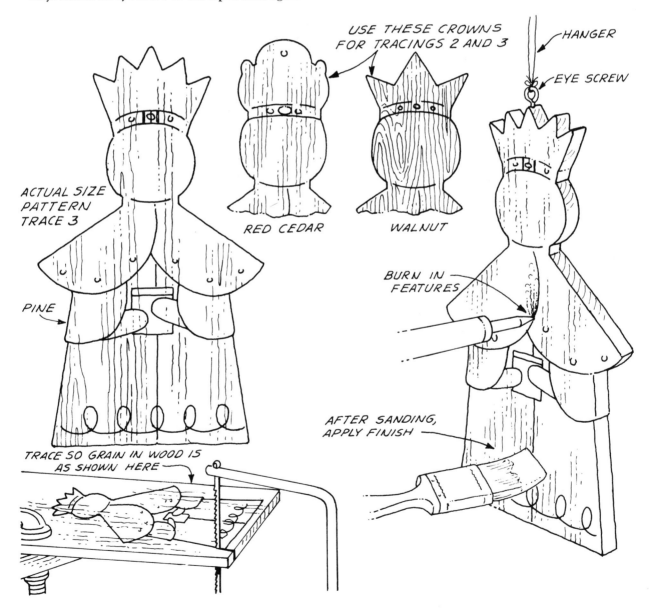

HENNY-PENNY CHICKEN

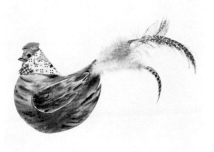

Balsa wood strip (⅛ inch thick x 4 inches wide)
Pencil
X-acto knife
Small brush
Small tube of burnt umber acrylic paint

Small tube of cadmium red acrylic paint
Cement
Feathers (2 for each bird)
Calico
Ornament hanger

Trace the pattern onto the balsa wood and cut it out very carefully with the knife. Balsa splits easily, so work slowly. There will be a rough edge like feathers. Cut out the wings. Paint a feather design on the wings and the chicken body; paint eyes on both sides. Add water to the paint for a lighter color if it appears too dark. Cut 4 triangles, each about ¼ inch long, from the balsa scraps. Glue 2 triangles under each wing to make the wings stand out from

the body. Glue on the wings. With the point of the knife make 2 small holes for the feathers. Dip the quill ends of the feathers in glue and insert for a tail.

Fold a small square of calico into a triangle and glue it around the chicken's neck for a scarf. Carefully pierce a small hole at the top of the figure's head for the hanger.

Contributed by Mrs. Anne Warlow
Reston, Virginia

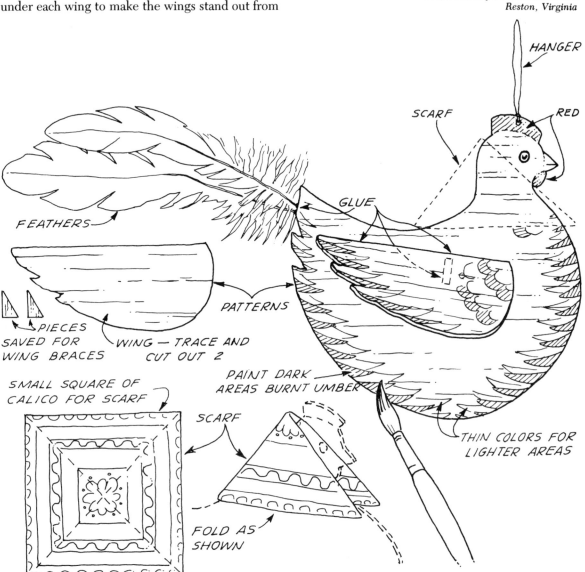

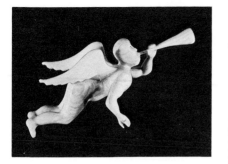

WOOD CARVING MADE SIMPLE

Pencil
Soft wood (white pine, balsa, etc.)
Coping saw
Razor knife
Sandpaper

Draw or trace a design on the wood. Using a coping saw, cut out the object. The razor knife is for rounding the edges and for making the features of the figure. Use the sandpaper for smoothing and shaping the wood.

Contributed by Mr. John Watts
Newport News, Virginia

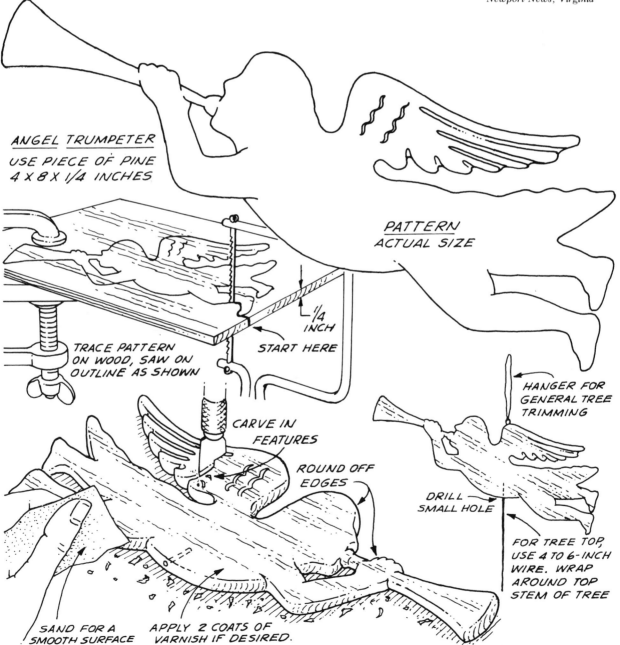

ANGEL TRUMPETER
USE PIECE OF PINE
4 X 8 X 1/4 INCHES

PATTERN
ACTUAL SIZE

1/4 INCH

START HERE

TRACE PATTERN ON WOOD, SAW ON OUTLINE AS SHOWN

CARVE IN FEATURES

ROUND OFF EDGES

HANGER FOR GENERAL TREE TRIMMING

DRILL SMALL HOLE

FOR TREE TOP, USE 4 TO 6-INCH WIRE. WRAP AROUND TOP STEM OF TREE

SAND FOR A SMOOTH SURFACE

APPLY 2 COATS OF VARNISH IF DESIRED.

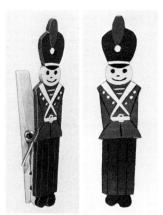

CLOTHESPIN SOLDIER

Large tongue depressor or piece of
 wood ⅛ inch thick
Pencil
X-acto knife or coping saw with a fine
 blade
Sandpaper

Blue, red, black, pink, white, and
 yellow enamel model paints
Fine brush
Medium brush
Household cement
Spring-type clothespin

Trace the pattern onto the wood and cut out using the X-acto knife or coping saw. Sandpaper the edges smooth. Draw on the details of the uniform very lightly with the pencil. Paint, letting the soldier dry thoroughly between layers.

Glue the clothespin to the back of the soldier so that the fastening end of the clothespin is even with the feet of the soldier.

NOTE: A variety of uniforms may be obtained by changing the colors.

Contributed by Mrs. Susan H. Rountree
Williamsburg, Virginia

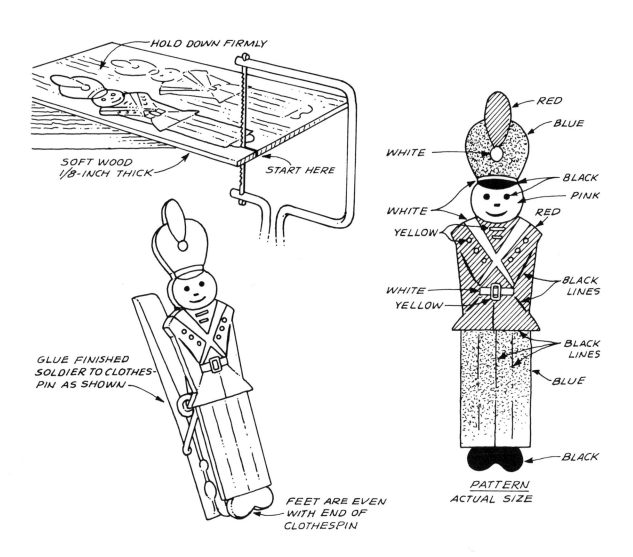

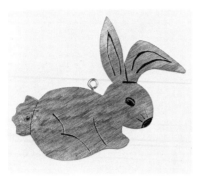

WOODEN SILHOUETTE ANIMAL

Pencil
White pine or any soft wood, 4 inches
    wide x ¼ inch thick
Coping saw, 32 teeth per inch
Medium sandpaper

Electric burning needle
Eye screw
Clear finish
Brush
Lightweight clear plastic fishing line

Trace the outline of a figure onto the wood and cut it out with a coping saw fitted with a fine blade. Sand the edges and both sides of the figure. Burn in features on both sides of the figure with an electric burning needle. Attach an eye screw to the top.

Apply 2 coats of clear finish. String fishing line through the eye screw for a hanger.

NOTE: Different types of wood will produce animals of different colors.

Contributed by Mr. William Blair
Williamsburg, Virginia

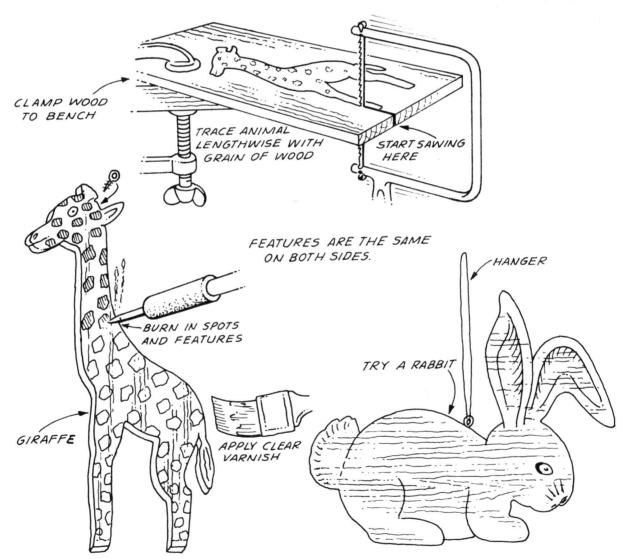

CLAMP WOOD TO BENCH

TRACE ANIMAL LENGTHWISE WITH GRAIN OF WOOD

START SAWING HERE

FEATURES ARE THE SAME ON BOTH SIDES.

HANGER

BURN IN SPOTS AND FEATURES

TRY A RABBIT

GIRAFFE

APPLY CLEAR VARNISH

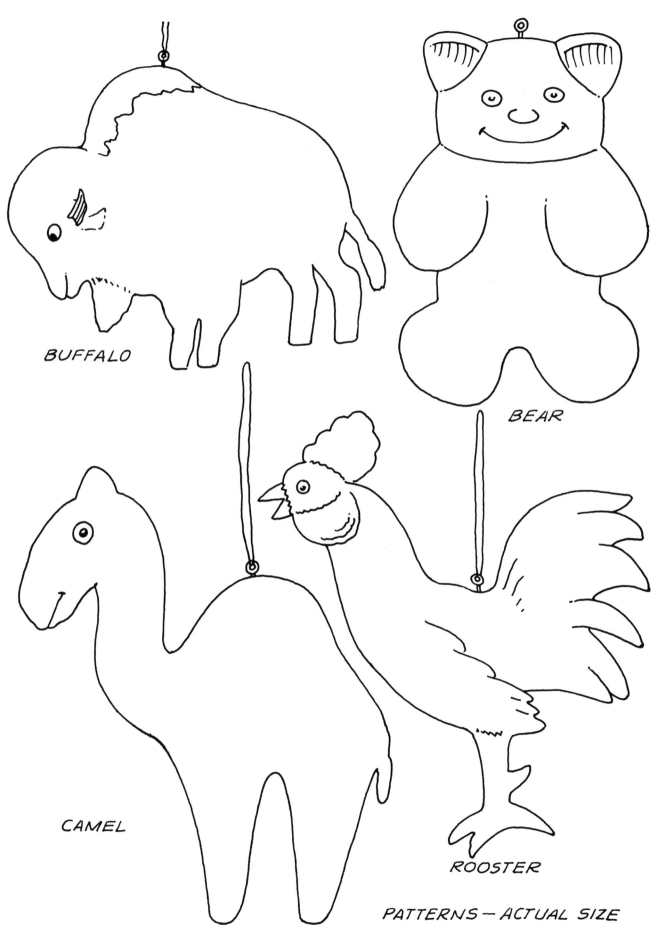

BUFFALO

BEAR

CAMEL

ROOSTER

PATTERNS — ACTUAL SIZE

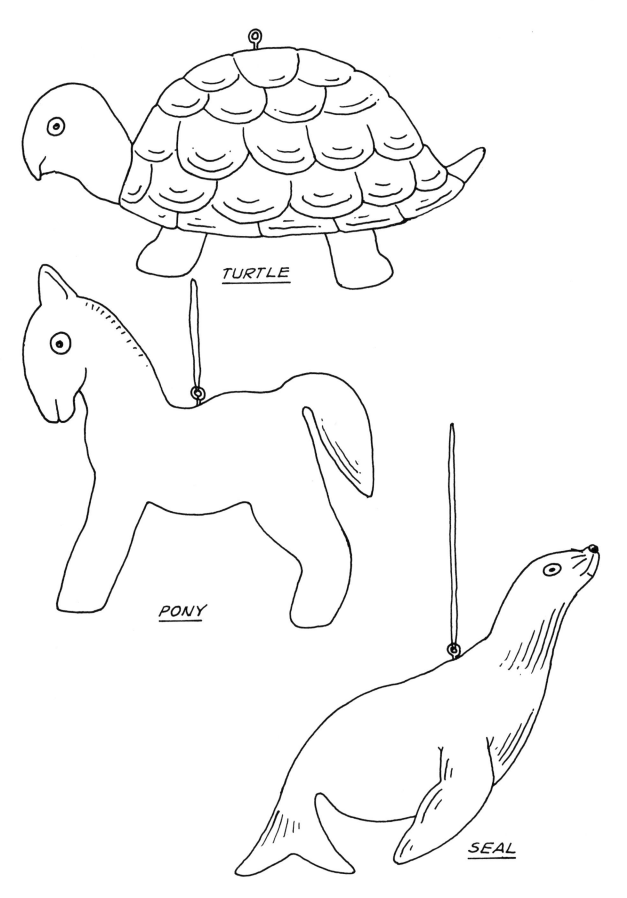

TURTLE

PONY

SEAL

PATTERNS - ACTUAL SIZE

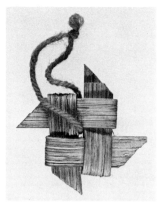

MOUNTAIN WHEEL STAR

Thin, freshly cut oak splint (1 splint
   20 inches long x ½ inch wide makes
   1 star)
Strong scissors or clippers

Water
Orange shellac
White glue
Red or green yarn, 6 inches long

Cut the freshly cut oak splint into 5-inch lengths and soak them in water about ½ hour to make them pliable. Carefully bend each of the 4 pieces in half over your second and third fingers so that they resemble hairpins. Wrap each loop around the open ends of the adjacent 1, slipping the fourth set of ends into the closed loop of the first 1. Cut a diagonal tip on each ray with the scissors. Press to interlock firmly and allow to dry completely. As the ornament shrinks, press it together tightly. When the star is completely dry, coat it with orange shellac. When the shellac is dry, drop a little glue in the center to keep the star from slipping apart. Cut a 6-inch piece of yarn and put it through the center of the star. Tie a knot in the yarn at the ends and hang the star from the tree.

Contributed by Mrs. William Galloway
Hampton, Virginia

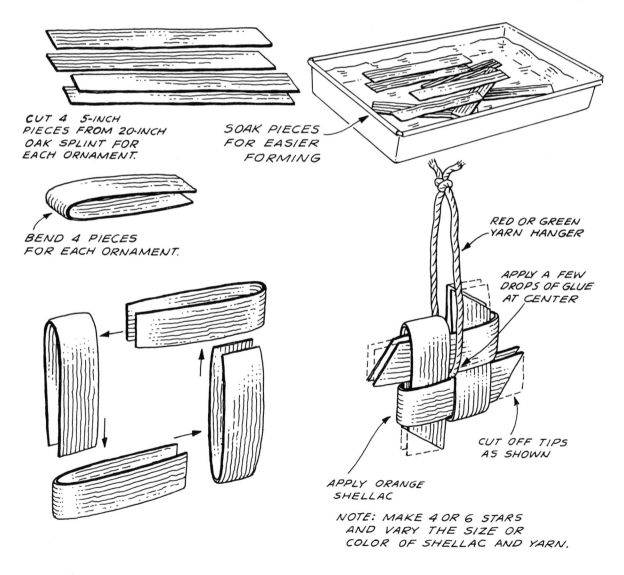

CUT 4 5-INCH PIECES FROM 20-INCH OAK SPLINT FOR EACH ORNAMENT.

SOAK PIECES FOR EASIER FORMING

BEND 4 PIECES FOR EACH ORNAMENT.

RED OR GREEN YARN HANGER

APPLY A FEW DROPS OF GLUE AT CENTER

CUT OFF TIPS AS SHOWN

APPLY ORANGE SHELLAC

NOTE: MAKE 4 OR 6 STARS AND VARY THE SIZE OR COLOR OF SHELLAC AND YARN.

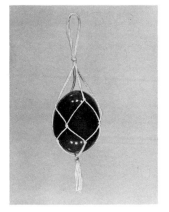

BLOWN EGG IN MACRAMÉ HOLDER

Water
Raw egg
Long straight pin or needle
Bowl
Red enamel model paint
Medium brush

Egg carton (for drying the egg)
3 yards of white mercerized heavy
　crochet cotton
Clipboard (to hold string)
Ruler

Wash the egg and dry thoroughly. With the pin or needle pierce a small hole in both ends of the shell. Hold the egg over the bowl and blow hard into the hole in the small end of the egg. Be sure to get all of the egg out of its shell. Puncturing the yolk will help. Run water through the empty shell, then let it dry completely.

Paint the shell with red enamel model paint and let it dry in an egg carton.

Divide 3 yards of heavy crochet cotton into 4 strands. Make a knot in the center. Double over and place in the clipboard. Knot 8 strands 2 inches down. Divide them into 4 groups of 2 strands each; knot each set 3 inches down. Taking 1 strand from 2 adjacent knots, knot together 1 inch down. Repeat all around. Continue for 2 more rows as shown. The end is formed by knotting all the strands ½ inch below the last row of knots, leaving the tail the length that you desire.

Place the dry painted egg in the macramé holder and hang it from the tree.

Contributed by Pompey Hollow Peaches 4-H Club
Cazenovia, New York

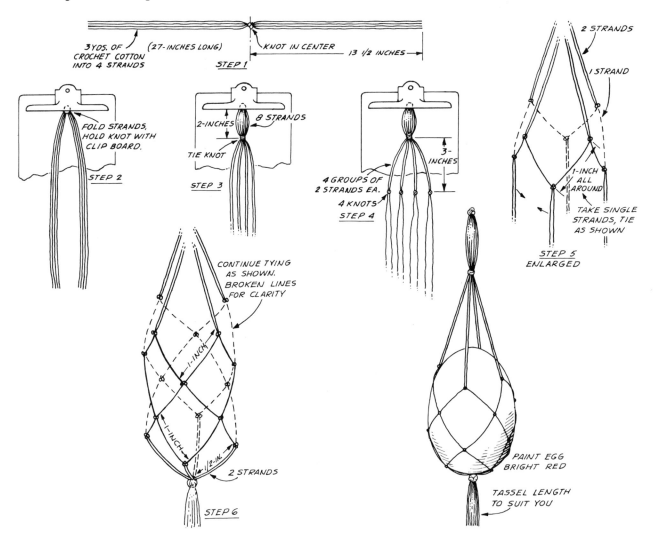

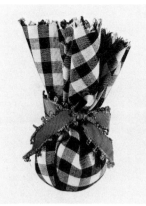

GINGHAM BAG WITH CLOVES

Small-checked gingham cloth
Pinking shears
100 whole cloves
Picot or other ribbon, ½ inch wide
and 10 inches long

With the pinking shears cut a piece of gingham cloth into a circle 8 inches in diameter. Place about 100 cloves in the center of the cloth and gather the ends of the material up to form a sack with the cloves inside it.

Tie the ribbon tightly in a bow around the neck of the sack. Add a hanger.

Contributed by Ms. Ann Brown
Williamsburg, Virginia

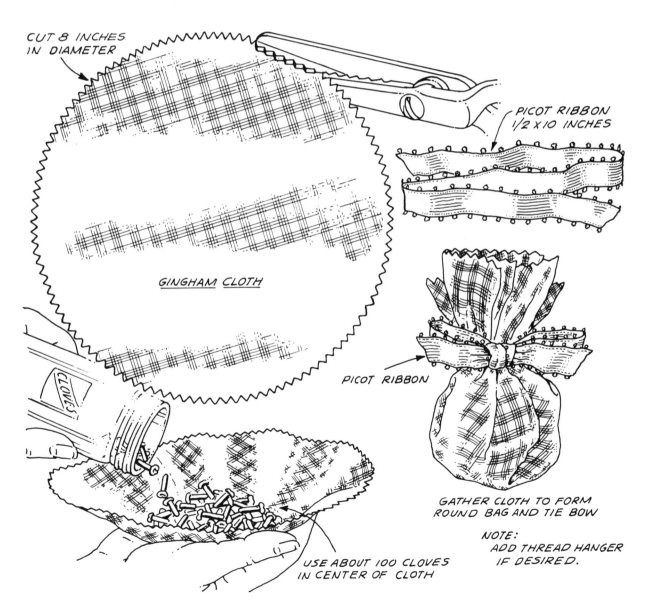

CUT 8 INCHES
IN DIAMETER

PICOT RIBBON
1/2 X 10 INCHES

GINGHAM CLOTH

CLOVES

PICOT RIBBON

GATHER CLOTH TO FORM
ROUND BAG AND TIE BOW

NOTE:
ADD THREAD HANGER
IF DESIRED.

USE ABOUT 100 CLOVES
IN CENTER OF CLOTH

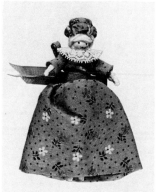

CLOTHESPIN DOLL

White glue
⅝-inch wooden bead
Round clothespin
Flesh, black, white, and red model
   paints
2 small brushes
Scissors
Eyelet lace
White fabric
Sewing needle
White thread
Pipe cleaner

Small print fabric
Matching thread
Straight pins
Yarn—yellow, brown, or black
Paper towel or tissue
Trim lace
Contrasting ribbon, ¼ inch wide x 12
   inches long
Lightweight clear plastic fishing line
Optional—small basket or paper
   flowers

Glue the ⅝-inch wooden bead to the top of the clothespin for a head. Let dry. Paint the face flesh color and allow to dry before adding the features.

Underclothing—Pantalets: Glue a short eyelet band (cut 2) around each leg. Glue a white band (cut 1) above the eyelet. Slip: Using pattern, cut white material, turn the edge under ⅛ inch, and sew on lace at the hem. Seam at the sides. Turn the slip to the right side and gather at the top for a waistband. Put the slip on the doll, pull the gathers to fit, and tie securely.

Arms—Wrap a pipe cleaner around the top of the clothespin for arms. Turn the ends under to form hands.

Dress—Using the top pattern, place the shoulders on the fold of the material, pin, and cut out. Sew the sides and underarm seams and turn to the right side. Cut a very small slit at the neck and slip the dress over the doll's head. Slip the doll's arms into the sleeves and tuck the edges of the sleeves under so that her hands stick out.

Using the pattern, cut out the skirt, seam sides, and hem. Use a double thread to gather the waist. Wrong side out, slip the skirt over the doll's head. Pull the waist tight and tie securely. Flip the skirt down so that it is right side out.

Hair—Use a few inches of yarn for hair. Starting at the top, glue the yarn down and around the face, leaving the back of the head bare.

Hat—Using the pattern, cut out the hat and turn the edge under on the line as shown. Hold it in place with a running stitch. Draw up the thread to form the hat. Stuff the hat with soft paper and glue it to the bead head and hair.

Neck—Run a drawstring through the trim lace and tie it around the doll's neck. Tie on a ribbon sash.

Finishing—Tie a small piece of fishing line around the doll's waist for a hanger. Flowers or a basket can be put in the doll's hands.

Contributed by Mrs. Barbara Hansford
Newport News, Virginia

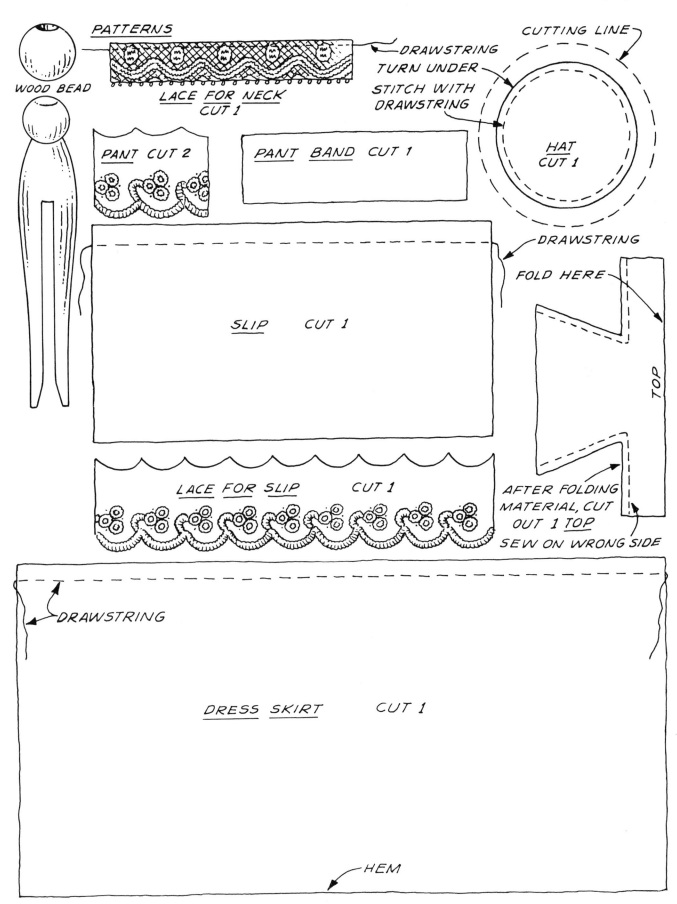

PATTERNS

WOOD BEAD

LACE FOR NECK
CUT 1

DRAWSTRING
TURN UNDER

STITCH WITH
DRAWSTRING

CUTTING LINE

HAT
CUT 1

PANT CUT 2

PANT BAND CUT 1

DRAWSTRING

FOLD HERE

TOP

SLIP   CUT 1

LACE FOR SLIP   CUT 1

AFTER FOLDING
MATERIAL, CUT
OUT 1 TOP
SEW ON WRONG SIDE

DRAWSTRING

DRESS SKIRT   CUT 1

HEM

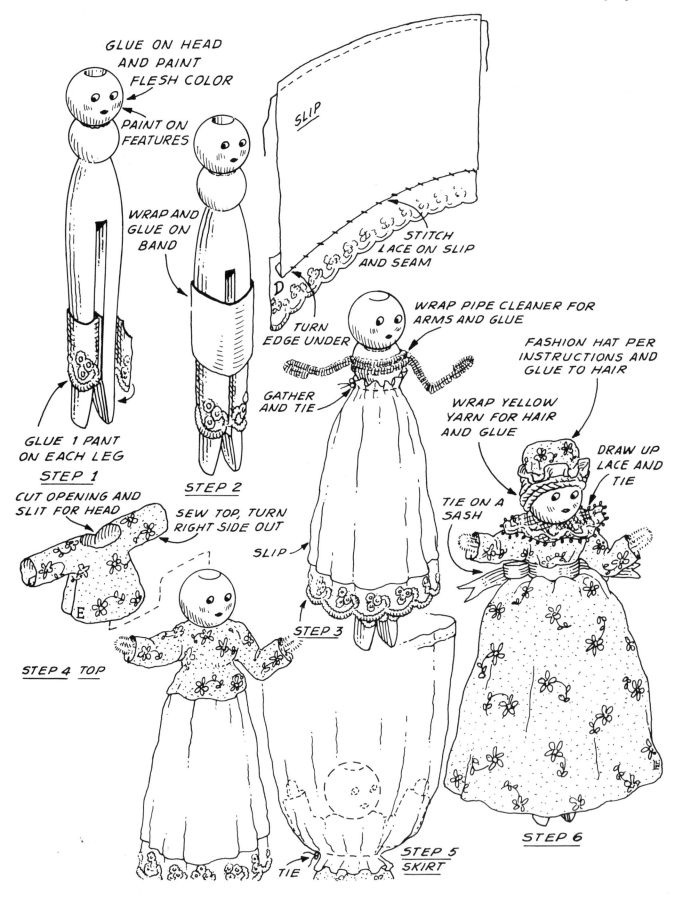

GLUE ON HEAD
AND PAINT
FLESH COLOR

PAINT ON
FEATURES

WRAP AND
GLUE ON
BAND

SLIP

STITCH
LACE ON SLIP
AND SEAM

TURN
EDGE UNDER

GLUE 1 PANT
ON EACH LEG

STEP 1

GATHER
AND TIE

WRAP PIPE CLEANER FOR
ARMS AND GLUE

FASHION HAT PER
INSTRUCTIONS AND
GLUE TO HAIR

WRAP YELLOW
YARN FOR HAIR
AND GLUE

DRAW UP
LACE AND
TIE

TIE ON A
SASH

STEP 2

CUT OPENING AND
SLIT FOR HEAD

SEW TOP, TURN
RIGHT SIDE OUT

SLIP

E

STEP 4 TOP

STEP 3

TIE

STEP 5
SKIRT

STEP 6

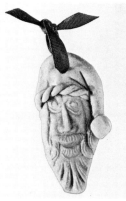

MOLDED SALT DOUGH ORNAMENT

Nonporous object with a simple
low-relief design (any raised image
on a glass, ceramic, or metal object
can be used) or a butter mold
Liquid cooking oil
Acrylic dental impression material
(available from a dental supply
company)

Flour
Salt
Water
Sharp knife
Polyurethane varnish
Brush
Red or green ribbon, ¼ inch wide

Choose a simple low-relief design on a nonporous metal, such as a face, flower, or geometric medallion on a glass, ceramic, or metal container, which you would like to copy in salt dough. A simple design can be released easily from the molding material. Lightly grease the design, then make a mold with the acrylic dental impression material, mixing according to the directions on the package. Or eliminate the mold-making process by selecting a butter mold instead.

Mix together 4 cups of flour, 1 cup of salt, and 1½ cups of water. Knead about 10 minutes on a floured surface until the dough is smooth. Add a little water if the dough is too stiff; add flour if it is too sticky. Cover the dough and refrigerate until used.

Grease the mold well with the liquid cooking oil, making sure that it does not obscure any details. Press enough dough into the mold to make an ornament about ½ inch in thickness. Remove the ornament from the mold slowly and carefully. Grease the mold each time that you use it. Trim the

edges of the molded ornament and accentuate details with a sharp knife. Attach any hand-formed embellishments, such as the hat and trim on the Bellarmine ornament, by slightly moistening the joint with water and pressing together.

Punch a hole in the top of each decoration with a sharp object. Bake in a 300° oven for 1½ hours or until the ornaments are golden and hard. Cool. Apply several coats of polyurethane varnish as a preservative.

NOTE: The recipe makes a large quantity of salt dough, which can be used to make free-form coils and braids. You can also make cookie cutter ornaments from it.

HISTORY: This salt dough Santa face was taken from a bearded face on a seventeenth-century German stoneware Bellarmine bottle. A hand-formed hat with a twisted trim was added to complete the decoration.

Contributed by Ms. Merry Abbitt
Williamsburg, Virginia

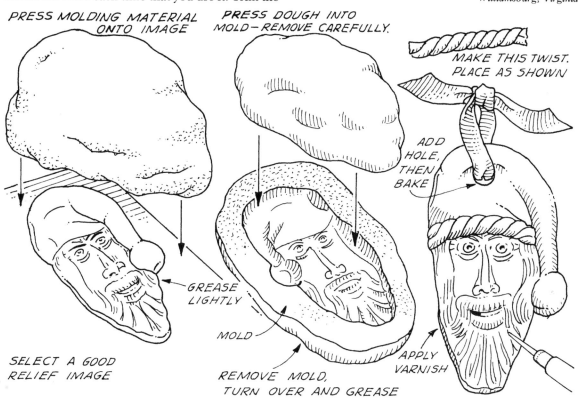